DAVID BOWIE OUTLAW

This book explores the relevance of David Bowie's life and music for contemporary legal and cultural theory. Focusing on the artist and artworks of David Bowie, this book brings to life, in essay form, particular theoretical ideas, creative methodologies and ethical debates that have contemporary relevance within the fields of law, social theory, ethics and art. What unites the essays presented here is that they all point to a beyond law: to the fact that law is not enough, or to be more precise, too much, too much to bear. For those who, like Bowie, see art, creativity and love as what ought to be the central organising principles of life, law will not do. In the face of its certainties, its rigidities, and its conceits, these essays, through Bowie, call forth the monster who laughs at the law, celebrate inauthenticity as a deeper truth, explore the ethical limits of art, cut up the laws of writing and embrace that which is most antithetical to law, love. This original engagement with the limits of law will appeal to those working in legal theory, ethics and law and popular culture, as well as in art and cultural studies.

Alex Sharpe is a professor of law at the University of Warwick. She is the author of *Sexual Intimacy and Gender Identity 'Fraud'* (Routledge, 2018), *Foucault's Monsters and the Challenge of Law* (Routledge, 2010) and *Transgender Jurisprudence* (Cavendish, 2002).

DAVID BOWIE OUTLAW

Essays on Difference, Authenticity, Ethics, Art & Love

Alex Sharpe

Routledge
Taylor & Francis Group

LONDON AND NEW YORK

First published 2022
by Routledge
2 Park Square, Milton Park, Abingdon, Oxon OX14 4RN

and by Routledge
605 Third Avenue, New York, NY 10158

Routledge is an imprint of the Taylor & Francis Group, an informa business

© 2022 Alex Sharpe

British Library Cataloguing-in-Publication Data
A catalogue record for this book is available from the British Library

Library of Congress Cataloging-in-Publication Data
A catalog record for this book has been requested

ISBN: 978-0-367-69104-2 (hbk)
ISBN: 978-0-367-69106-6 (pbk)
ISBN: 978-1-003-14042-9 (ebk)

DOI: 10.4324/9781003140429

Typeset in Bembo
by Apex CoVantage, LLC

For Anne, who has taught me much about difference, authenticity, ethics, art and love.

CONTENTS

Foreword		*ix*
Preface		*xi*
Acknowledgements		*xiii*
Introduction		1
Difference		**11**
1	Law's monsters: the hopeful undecidability of David Bowie	13
	Introduction 13	
	A monster framework 14	
	The hopefulness of monsters 16	
	Bowie as hopeful monster 17	
	Bowie and gender/sexual ambiguity 18	
	Conclusion 20	
Authenticity		**25**
2	Authenticity: what a drag!	27
	Introduction 27	
	On authenticity 28	
	Subverting (artistic) authenticity 29	
	Conclusion 34	

Ethics 39

3 'Flirting' with fascism: the Thin White Duke, art
and ethical limits 41
Introduction 41
An ethical framework for evaluating artworks 42
The Thin White Duke and fascism 45
Judging Bowie's artwork 49
Conclusion 51

Art 57

4 Cutting up the laws of writing: the Burroughs effect 59
Introduction 59
Cutting up Burroughs 60
Before Burroughs: the dreamscape 62
After Burroughs: accelerating the process 62
Diamond Dogs *63*
Conclusion 66

Love 71

5 Bowie love: beyond law 73
Introduction 73
Escaping necessity 75
Love as letting go 76
Love as humility 77
Love as posthuman 79

References 85
Index 99

FOREWORD

David Bowie Outlaw undoubtedly belongs with those few great texts on music that are equal to the wild glories that inspired their creation. You need to be a great act to pull off a thesis as bold as this: Bowie is a law giver. But, before the house lights go down, we need to rid ourselves of some preconceptions about this word. Read or heard through Bowie, law is what binds us to something: a fascination, a message, an invitation to venture forth. We bind ourselves. Most philosophy of law has forgotten this fundamental truth.

Now, the theatre is shaking, the band is tuning up, a strip of white lights illuminates the stage. Who/what is it that comes? Sharpe's Bowie enters through the arch of the 'now.' She/he/they are the will to reaffirm life, as a unique grasping of its own creative potential. This moment of affirmation is the 'law' that the book evokes: the singular way in which Bowie's music enters its listener and transfers or transmits a power. Of course, this power slips away as it is summoned, and it is this peculiar ethics that Sharpe's Bowie evokes. Only the irreplaceable can be lost. In the face of this truth, the strong reader/listener creates and fails again.

Sharpe's book is as perfectly formed as a Mick Ronson riff. It's like the build from Suffragette City, funnelling and intensifying its own energies. This is the message that runs through Ziggy Stardust, Aladdin Sane and the Thin White Duke: the artist has to destroy her own creation to kindle the energies that will allow further invention. Creative thought is a kaleidoscope, re-arranging its own patterns, twisting and turning upon itself, making itself anew. This book is a kaleidoscope – an experiment in white magic – a talisman to ward off boredom, fascists and gravity.

Bowie as outlaw: Bowie is a law giver, but unlike most law givers, Bowie's law destroys the law: the only command is 'create afresh.' True creation is not narcissism. Sharpe's Bowie is a figure of ethics, or a spirit that knows its own wealth must be constantly squandered. The real artist, then, is entirely anonymous, merely a conduit for energies from elsewhere that seek their receivers and transmitters.

Ultimately, for every grave Apollo, there is a laughing gnome – a goblin voiced Dionysus. While Baal so wisely pointed out that nothing is so hard as the quest for fun, creativity has its joyous methods. Sharpe's understanding of Nietzschean normativity is thus to listen to the multitudes within, to follow the arcs of their/our transformation. This is not philosophy, this is not jurisprudence, this is a genocide of old ideas and dead forms. Here is the secret Sharpe shares with us: We are Bowie.

Adam Gearey
Professor of Law,
Birkbeck College,
University of London   May 2021

PREFACE

This book owes its genesis, not to a clearly thought-out plan but to that well-spring of so many creative possibilities including Bowie's own, happenstance. In 2016, shortly after Bowie's death, I was approached by Arizona State University (ASU) and invited to keynote a humanities conference organised around the theme of monsters. Monsters were very much in the academic air at the time due to the then upcoming bicentenary of Mary Shelley's Frankenstein novel (1818). The invite was quite out of the blue, and attributable to the impact of my second book, *Foucault's Monsters and the Challenge of Law*, published in 2010 with Routledge.

After discussing the parameters of my invited lecture, ASU made it clear I had an almost free hand regarding its content provided I addressed the theme of monsters. As I began to think about my focus and to write the lecture through February and March 2016, I was simultaneously listening to a lot of Bowie's music, including music I had not listened to for a long time. At first, given the recency of his death, it proved a bitter-sweet experience, but Bowie quickly insinuated himself into the project. Before long, I looked and frowned, and the monster, ASUs monster, was Bowie. After all, who better than Bowie to exemplify the hybridity of the monster? And so, the ASU lecture began to take shape. Moreover, with Bowie on board, the possibilities quickly multiplied. While the lecture remained an academic affair, it became, through Bowie, an audio-visual event, a piece of performance. Moreover, the Phoenix lecture became a catalyst for a lecture tour. Thus, earlier versions of what would ultimately become the first essay in this collection were delivered in several Australian and UK cities during 2016–2018.

At this stage, I did not intend to write a book. However, in 2019, I was invited to present a public lecture on Bowie at the fifth Dublin David Bowie Festival 2020. As I was already working on an article on the influence of William Burroughs on Bowie for the Cut-Ups@60 conference organised by the European Beat Studies Network, I decided to present a version of this article in lecture form in Dublin, again accompanied by sound and vision care of Bowie. The development of this article/lecture ultimately became the fourth essay in this collection. The writing of the remaining three essays, which address ideas of authenticity, ethics and love, and the decision to present all of the material in book form took place during the first Covid-19 pandemic lockdown and its aftermath. Indeed, during this period, authenticity, ethics and love, while abiding concerns, seemed to take on heightened significance for our individual and collective lives. As with monsters and Burroughs' cut-ups writing technique, Bowie again proved a perfect conduit for conveying these ideas. During the period March through to September, while cocooning with Bowie, I completed a first full draft of the book. At times, when writing this book, it has felt like I am channelling Bowie, that he is writing through me. However, the aim of the book has been to write through him, to use him to distil the essence of things and to give things a sense of immediacy, something which Bowie always managed to do with aplomb through his music and art.

ACKNOWLEDGEMENTS

In writing this collection of essays, I have received the support, encouragement and constructive criticism of many friends and colleagues. In particular, I would like to thank Sharon Cowan, John Danaher, Berys Gaut, Oliver Harris, Les Moran, Alan Norrie, Anthony Wrigley, Gary Watt and Aleardo Zanghellini. The collection of essays has also benefited from the comments of various audiences. The first essay, 'Law's monsters: the hopeful undecidability of David Bowie,' has benefited from comments of audiences at public lectures given in Phoenix, Canberra, Brisbane, London (2016), Manchester, Keele, Edinburgh (2017) and Sheffield (2018). The London event, 'Bowie at Birkbeck,' held at Birkbeck Cinema, proved to be particularly helpful as my lecture was part of a series of events organised around Bowie which led to some really engaging conversations with other invited speakers, discussants and audience members. I would particularly like to thank Daniel Monk for organising this event and Piyel Haldar and Adam Gearey for their thoughtful engagement. The fourth essay, 'Cutting up the laws of writing: the Burroughs effect,' has benefited from comments of the audience at the fifth annual David Bowie Festival in Dublin (2020) and from the Q&A with Tony Visconti and Woody Woodmansey. I would also like to thank John Brereton, the festival organiser, for inviting me to participate in the festival in both 2020 and 2021. The third essay, "Flirting' with fascism: the Thin White Duke, art and ethical limits,' has benefited from comments of the audience at a public lecture at the University of Warwick (2021). I acknowledge the following copyright permission. An earlier version of the first essay appears as 'Scary monsters: the hopeful undecidability of David Bowie 1947–2016' in *Law and Humanities* (2017) reprinted by permission of Taylor and Francis Ltd www.tandfonline.com And finally, special thanks to Cartoon Bowie for the cover art.

INTRODUCTION

This book contains a collection of five essays. Each will bring to life, through the artist and artworks of David Bowie, a particular theoretical idea, creative methodology or ethical debate that has contemporary relevance within the fields of law, social theory, ethics and/or art. What unites the essays is that they all point to a beyond law. To the fact that law is not enough, or to be more precise, too much, too much to bear. For those who, like Bowie, see art, creativity and love as what ought to be the central organising principles of life, law will not do. In the face of its certainties, its rigidities, and its conceits, the essays, through Bowie, call forth the monster who laughs at the law, celebrate inauthenticity as a deeper truth, explore the ethical limits of art, cut up the laws of writing and embrace that which is most antithetical to law, love.

The essays are written so as to be accessible to non-academic as well as academic audiences. In one sense, the approach adopted is similar to Slavoj Zizek's use of the films of Alfred Hitchcock as a means to explain the complex psychoanalytical ideas of Jacques Lacan.[1] As a form of public engagement, the essays adopt a more informal, and at times playful style, in contrast to the usual protocols of academic writing. In flouting conventions of genre, they become alive to their subject matter. That is, they become monstrous or, which is the same thing, Bowiesque. The essays, which have various points of connection, consider the themes of difference (to be explored through the figure of the outsider par excellence, the monster) and authenticity (especially its artistic variant), the relationship between art and ethics (to be explored through Bowie's artistic 'flirtation' with fascism in the mid-1970s), creative methods (to be explored through Bowie's use of William Burroughs' cut-ups writing method) and love (specifically, *agape*, a Greco-Christian idea capturing the idea of a love for humanity).

The aim is to explore particular ideas, creative methods and debates through Bowie, rather than making Bowie the object of writing. This can be contrasted

DOI: 10.4324/9781003140429-1

with a significant and growing literature that focuses on Bowie himself and the impact of his work. Most of this work is biographical in nature.[2] However, more recent interdisciplinary academic work that considers Bowie also tends to focus on the man, on the significance of his art and music, and on the wider influence it has had on music, art and popular culture, rather than using him as a means (a guide) to explore particular ideas and/or issues.[3] For example, the editors of *Enchanting David Bowie: Space Time Body Memory*[4] explain their book "reflect[s] upon the cultural and artistic significance of David Bowie,"[5] while the editors of *David Bowie: Critical Perspectives* highlight their aim to:

> engage critically with one of the most enduring, intriguing and complex figures within popular culture and to add to the emerging academic debate which seeks to assess Bowie's significance as a songwriter, performer, recording artist, music producer, actor, film producer and painter.[6]

Will Brooker focuses on "the structures, themes and motifs that run through Bowie's work"[7] but again the aim is to "[discover] what they tell us about Bowie in all his forms,"[8] while in his most recent book, *Why Bowie Matters*,[9] Bowie is necessarily centre stage. Further, in relation to the subject matter of the present collection of essays it is only the theme of authenticity that has, in different ways and to different degrees, received sustained academic attention within this broader literature.[10]

Moreover, and in contrast to this book, these and other academic contributions, perhaps unsurprisingly, are, at least in the main, written in a style not easily accessible to non-academic audiences. Simon Critchley's *Bowie* is an exception here.[11] It is a very accessible book written by a distinguished philosopher. However, while it is full of important philosophical insights, and in this respect, I am indebted to him, Critchley's *Bowie* is very much written from the perspective of a fan and is, in many respects, autobiographical, mapping the impact of Bowie on a single life. While it touches on some of the themes to be developed in this book, most notably, the themes of authenticity and love, Critchley does not present either idea in the form of a developed argument in his *Bowie* text.

Why Bowie? That is, why draw on Bowie as the conduit through which to explore and render accessible particular ideas? Apart from the fact he "always felt like a vehicle for something else,"[12] Bowie is an appropriate choice because he (or at least some of his personas) is well known, and he is a widely loved artist. This makes him an excellent, indeed seductive hook for readers, who are likely to have at least some degree of familiarity with his work. Moreover, Bowie is a particularly significant artist of the late twentieth and early twenty-first centuries. As early as 1971, the *New York Times* recognised him to be "the most intellectually brilliant man yet to choose the long-playing album as his medium of expression."[13] Indeed, Bowie, almost single-handedly, transformed rock 'n' roll into an unlimited form of expression. His "rare ability to synthesise avant-garde ideas"[14] and present them in a form that resonates with more general audiences led music critic, Howard Goodall, to characterise Bowie as a 'second wave' composer,[15] akin to Bach, Mozart or

Beethoven. More than any other creative figure within popular culture, it is perhaps Bowie who has entered our collective psyche and whose death has triggered the greatest sense of collective loss.

As Devereux, Dillane and Power put it, there has never "been an artist as intellectually, musically and visually compelling, as David Bowie."[16] How true. In both life and death, he seemed able to transform experience into art. Moreover, and while Bowie is so much more than the music, an example from the world of music is instructive because music is, as Jacques Attali contends, prophecy. It "makes audible the new world that will gradually become visible,"[17] or as Bowie has put it: "[t]omorrow belongs to those who hear it coming."[18] More particularly, Bowie is an ideal figure because his considerable body of work addresses, and in a sustained way, subject matter that continues to interest us in non-trivial ways: the figure of the outsider,[19] the ethical boundaries of art, the importance of love, as well as other abiding concerns. He was also both a curator and critic of contemporary culture, offering us a series of mirrors through which to glimpse society and ourselves. So, it will be Bowie, rightly acknowledged to be the first postmodern rock star,[20] who will be our guide.

Before proceeding to detail the contents of the essays that follow, it should be recognised that in writing about Bowie, or in the present context through Bowie, one has emotional investments. While Bowie had his critics,[21] nobody who has written about him in a serious and sustained way, whether academic[22] or music journalist,[23] has done so other than from a position marked by fandom. We are all tasteful fans. And, of course, Bowie himself was a life-long fan, that is, of the creative output of others, of succeeding generations of artists.[24] Like Picasso, he shared this child-like quality, this openness, this sense of not a little wonder. It is though, precisely such investments that make Bowie such an excellent vehicle for the essays as they are shared by millions of people.

However, the reader should note that in discussing particular ideas, creative methods and debates through Bowie, I will articulate arguments, take positions and offer interpretations which may or may not persuade and/or resonate. The aim here is not to provide definitive answers to important questions. If this were the aim, Bowie would clearly be the wrong vehicle. Rather, the aim of each essay is to render a particular idea, or set of ideas, more accessible. In each case, it is hoped the reader will be seduced to discover more,[25] in much the same way Bowie encouraged fans to explore, for example, Jacques Brel, Karl heinz Stockhausen, Erich Heckel, Wilhelm Reich and Yukio Mishima. Equally, readers, and especially Bowie aficionados, might take issue with some of my interpretations of Bowie. As the essays will make clear, this is perhaps not only inevitable, an effect of our situatedness and the indeterminacy of language coupled with Bowie's penchant for allusion and opacity. It should also be welcomed. After all, as will become clear, lack of consensus on Bowie serves only to demonstrate his importance. That is, while it can feel like he speaks to us individually ('I had to phone someone so I picked on you'),[26] his art and music address an emotional reservoir of difference.

The first essay in this collection, 'Law's monsters: the hopeful undecidability of David Bowie,' deals with the theme of *difference*. This theme has spawned an enormous academic literature, within and across continental philosophy,[27] feminism,[28] critical race theory,[29] queer theory,[30] trans theory,[31] critical disability studies[32] and postcolonial theory.[33] Bowie is clearly apposite here. After all, he occupied, nay celebrated, the position of the outsider. Think of his formal acting roles (Bowie was always in acting mode): alien (Nicholas Roeg's *The Man Who Fell to Earth*),[34] degenerate (Bertolt Brecht's *Baal* on the BBC),[35] vampire (*The Hunger*),[36] freak (*The Elephant Man* on Broadway)[37] as well as the off-screen characters he inhabited and performed: Ziggy, Aladdin Sane,[38] Halloween Jack, the Thin White Duke, Pierrot.

The outsider has many templates within social theory. Rene Girard's *scapegoat* and Zygmunt Bauman's *stranger* provide but two examples.[39] The first essay in this collection homes in on one, the legal and social outsider par excellence, the *monster*. It will consider the monster's social and legal constitution and its intrinsic hopefulness. As we will see, Bowie symbolised and embodied this figure, and the hope that lies at its core, in a variety of ways. He did so not only through transgressive art and music but through imagining and creating futures when it seemed repetitive tomorrows[40] would be our lot and because he pointed to the place of the sacred in a world without God. Through Bowie, the essay will consider the monster theories articulated by Georges Canguilhem[41] and Michel Foucault[42] which understand the appearance of monsters as the effect of a double breach, of nature and law. However, because, these theorists neglect the theme of hope, the essay will supplement their accounts with insights provided by Jacques Derrida, which foreground the monster/hope relationship.[43]

While there are other ways of understanding monsters,[44] the essay will focus on these authors because their accounts are, in my view, the most analytically precise and in the case of Canguilhem, and even more, so Foucault, offer the greatest explanatory power in terms of understanding how monsters come into the world and why they fade away. An example of a different approach to monsters is one that draws on psychoanalysis. Psychoanalysis understands the monster in universal terms. That is, we are all monsters, holes rather than wholes. As Jeffrey Cohen puts it: "[t]o be oedipalized, to become a speaking subject, is both to be born (as a unified being) and to die (to be torn apart, become monstrous)."[45] However, it remains the case that only some individuals or groups are, at any given historical moment, demonised or outcast by the term monster. Accordingly, it becomes important to inquire after the social and legal conditions through which monsters become culturally intelligible.

Moreover, while this and other essays in this collection will, at times, draw on psychoanalytical themes, the focus in relation to monsters, and indeed later essays (especially those dealing with ideas of authenticity and love), lies not with what is repressed and which may or may not be recovered but with the possibility of escape from, or reinvention of, our present selves. The aim is, as Critchley rightly points out, not the rediscovery of past selves from whom we were divided in infancy but something more protean and inventive. It is "to escape from being us."[46] Monsters call all kinds of distinctions into question. They are, as Cohen has pointed out, "harbinger[s] of category crisis."[47] For the purposes of this essay, however, and through Bowie, we will focus on distinctions of gender and sexuality in order to explore this theme.

The second essay, 'Authenticity: what a drag!,' will consider the idea of authenticity. It may seem odd to select Bowie for this purpose given music critics have repeatedly accused him of inauthenticity, of being a poseur, a phoney.[48] The essay will not attempt to counter these accusations. To do so would miss the point. After all, in the face of them, Bowie simply shrugged. Having embraced inauthenticity to powerful artistic effect what else could he do? Rather, following Simon Critchley,[49] the essay will highlight how the coupling of authenticity with truth, the special intimacy these two terms are generally thought to have within the wider culture and especially within rock music, is highly problematic. Through Bowie, the essay will argue that authenticity does not monopolise truth. At the very least, experiences of truth, especially in the artistic realm, span the in/authenticity divide.

However, the essay will make a stronger claim, namely, that inauthenticity reveals a deeper truth because inauthenticity is all there is, it is how we experience the world and ourselves, as fragmented, multitudinous, cacophonous. One of the reasons why David Bowie resonates with so many people is because of his ability to consistently acknowledge this complex reality, and our fragility, through his music and art. This essay will explain how Bowie subverted the idea of authenticity, especially its artistic variant. And it will consider how Bowie engaged with the world, not from the point of view of some deep personal truth that demands expression but through successive acts of self-creation, ones that drew voraciously on world culture, and it will highlight how, through an ambivalence concerning authorship and lyric meaning, Bowie helped constitute fans as active agents and creative communities.

The third essay, "Flirting' with fascism: the Thin White Duke, art and ethical limits,' foregrounds ethics in the context of evaluating the aesthetic value of transgressive art. Bowie's was transgressive in many ways, always exhibiting an interest in the darker side or under belly of social and psychic life. One outlet for this interest, one perhaps especially relevant to our political present, found artistic expression in his exploration of dystopias, past, present and particularly future. His conceptual album *The Rise and Fall of Ziggy Stardust and the Spiders from Mars*,[50] the later *Diamond Dogs*[51] (his musical version of George Orwell's *1984*) and *Outside*[52] stand out in this respect, though they fail to exhaust his interest. One particular theme Bowie explored is the relationship between leader (star) and followers (audience), especially those moments when the latter give themselves over to the former, to power. This theme reached its climax with Bowie's emotionally distant aristocratic character, the Thin White Duke, who, through performance and stagecraft,[53] conjured up images of Nuremberg rallies. Indeed, while the Duke, Bowie was accused of flirting with fascism.[54]

It is *this* Bowie, and the sublime[55] affect he had on audiences, that will provide the focus of this essay. In exploring the relationship between ethics, aesthetics and art, through the vehicle of Bowie's Duke, the essay will pose and seek to answer the following questions: (1) is the aesthetic value of an artwork conditioned by its ethical properties? (2) If so, is this true in all or only some contexts? and (3) Where true, does this mean ethically defective artworks are necessarily aesthetically diminished? In order to answer these questions, the essay will draw on three broad philosophical positions that consider the relationship between ethical and aesthetic values of art: *moralism*, *autonomism* and *immoralism*. The essay will offer a defence of Bowie's artwork through the lens of immoralism, and it will argue that in this context the answer to the third question is 'No.' Finally, because this essay deals with complex moral arguments and involves the making of a sustained argument about a particular artwork, it will be somewhat longer than the other essays in the collection.

In the fourth essay, 'Cutting up the laws of writing: the Burroughs effect,' we turn to the theme of *creativity*, which we will explore through the cut-ups writing method, beat writer, William Burroughs developed and helped popularise, whereby a written text (or texts) is/are cut up and rearranged to create a new text. Most obviously, the practice provides a framework for artists to kick-start their creativity, to overcome blockage. However, for Burroughs, it was also a weapon he deployed in his war against language. Through its linear narrative structure and syntactical rules, Burroughs viewed language – the word-virus – as having colonised 'us,' its host, and through this parasitic relationship, which is how he viewed human being, he understood our sense of internal coherence or identity to have taken shape.[56] Through cut-ups, Burroughs sought to challenge language's hold on our perceptions. Cut-ups, because they privilege the image over the word, enable us to see differently, to recognise patterns and rhythms of experience that otherwise remain hidden. They bring us closer to a felt reality.

Burroughs cut-ups method exerted considerable influence over a range of counter-cultural figures, especially in the world of rock 'n' roll.[57] The essay will focus on one of Burroughs' more notable offspring, David Bowie, for whom the adoption of cut-ups from 1974 on proved decisive in several ways. First, like other artists, Bowie used cut-ups as a creative trigger. They also enabled him to accelerate his output, "accommodating a mind that couldn't slow down"[58] and to sever his writing from the personal, the autobiographical. Cut-ups were the perfect solution for a tasteful thief who had a preference for the random and a reluctance to bear his artistic 'soul.' More importantly, however, cut-ups helped Bowie to convey the ineffable, that which cannot be captured in literal words, or at least to give an audience a heightened emotional experience. Cut-ups assist in producing this affect because words, which otherwise get in the way, are transformed into portraits, photographs, vignettes. Crucially, cut-ups, which confront, move beyond the laws of writing, contributed to some of Bowie's best, most affecting music, something the essay will explore through a focus on what I consider to be his best album, the vertigo-inducing, *Diamond Dogs*. As we will see, cut-ups, precluding an authoritative reading of lyrics as they do, enabled Bowie to convey creative agency on the listener who fills in the gaps with "[her] imagination, with [her] longing."[59]

In the final essay, 'Bowie love: beyond law,' we will consider Bowie as a philosopher of the wisdom of love[60] and, therefore, as a philosopher who grants priority to ethics (which centres otherness) over ontology or being (which centres self). The Bowie-love nexus to be considered concerns itself with *agape*, a Greco-Christian term capturing the idea of a love for humanity, a universal and unconditional love or at least a striving toward it. While *agape* might suggest the divine, the Bowie-love nexus to be developed here remains an earthly affair. It foregrounds Alain Badiou's distinction between identity and difference.[61] Like Badiou, Bowie sought to privilege difference over identity, mobile otherness over static selfhood, love over law. Indeed, Bowie always reconstructed the world through the filter of difference, not the difference of a specific love object (the beloved) or that of the couple (Badiou's "the two")[62] but through difference at large. And it was through these reconstructed worlds of sound and vision that he established affective relationships with fans.

Bowie love speaks to the freedom to become, to Foucault's "possibility of being otherwise,"[63] that is, to the possibility of being and living differently from what might otherwise be thought one's destiny. The love he fostered is founded on embracing freedom to be different and on embracing the warm impermanence of the manifestation of differences in ourselves and others. In the face of such a hopeful and loving path, however, stands ideology. Through otherworldly constructions and through showing us their seams, Bowie demystified the world, teased the ideological out into the open. It is the ideological, the social norms we have internalised, ones that insufficiently value difference, that hold us back, that make the possibility of love recede. It is to the undoing of these social norms, which parade as necessity, that Bowie directed his art. In this sense, Bowie's art addresses the very ground of and interconnection between love and freedom. In developing these ideas, this final essay will focus first on Bowie's subversion of social norms as a precondition of love/freedom. It will then turn to consider three important lessons evident in Bowie's work, one's that speak to love: love as letting go, love as humility and love as posthuman.

Notes

1   Žižek, 2010.
2   Buckley, 2005; Spitz, 2009; Doggett, 2011; Trynka, 2011; Leigh, 2014; Sheffield, 2016; Morley, 2016; Jones, 2018.
3   Devereux et al, 2015; Cinque et al, 2015; Waldrep, 2015; Ammon, 2016; Brooker, 2017; Brooker, 2019.
4   Cinque et al, 2015.
5   Cinque et al, 2015, p. 1.
6   Devereux et al, 2015, p. xiv.
7   Brooker, 2017, p. 7.
8   Brooker, 2017, preface.
9   Brooker, 2019.
10 See, for example, Usher and Fremaux, 2015; Reisch, 2016.
11 Critchley, 2014.

12 Miles, 1984, p. 23.
13 Erlich, 1971.
14 Johnson, 2015, p. 11.
15 Goodall, 2013, p. 165.
16 Devereux et al, 2015, p. xv.
17 Attali, 1985, p. 11.
18 This phrase was the slogan Bowie used to advertise his *Heroes* Album, 1977.
19 The theme of 'outsiderness' has played an important role in constituting Bowie-fan relationships. As noted by Toija Cinque and Sean Redmond, fans' relationships with Bowie are often "framed through culturally empowering narratives of gender and sexual transformation or around discourses of outsiderdom and alienation" from which "Bowie provided [an] escape . . . a 'home' to arrive in" (Cinque and Redmond, 2019, p. 41).
20 Savage, 2005. Jon Savage described Bowie's 1972 album, *The Rise and Fall of Ziggy Stardust and the Spiders from Mars* as the first postmodern record.
21 See, for example, Emerson (1974) and Bangs (1975).
22 Devereux et al, 2015; Cinque et al, 2015; Waldrep, 2015; Ammon, 2016; Brooker, 2017, 2019.
23 Buckley, 2005; Spitz, 2009; Doggett, 2011; Trynka, 2011; Leigh, 2014; Sheffield, 2016; Morley, 2016; Jones, 2018.
24 Indeed, this was one of the reasons Bowie drew so extensively on the creativity of other artists. As he stated, "I have to interplay with other writers, because I've always been a fan" (Shaar Murray, 1973).
25 It is for this reason an extensive list of references can be found at the end of this book.
26 'Starman' (*The Rise and Fall of Ziggy Stardust and the Spiders from Mars* album, 1972 RCA).
27 For example, Sartre, 2018; de Beauvoir, 1997; Levinas, 1999; Derrida, 2001; Foucault, 2003; Critchley, 2013.
28 For example, Kristeva, 1984; hooks, 1981; Irigaray, 1985; Spelman, 1988; MacKinnon, 1988; Young, 1990.
29 For example, Williams, 1992; Crenshaw et al, 1996; Delgado and Stefancic, 1998; Wilde, 2003.
30 For example, Butler, 1990; Sedgwick, 1990; Fuss, 1991; Butler, 1993; Warner, 1993.
31 For example, Prosser, 1998; Stryker and Whittle, 2006; Serano, 2007.
32 For example, McRuer, 2006; Kumari-Campbell, 2009; Kafer, 2013; Ellis et al, 2018.
33 For example, Fanon, 2020; Said, 2003; Landry, 1996.
34 The film, *The Man Who fell to Earth* (1976) is a British science fiction drama directed by Nicholas Roeg and distributed by British Lion Films.
35 Bowie played the part of Baal in a 1982 BBC television production of Bertolt Brecht's 1918 play.
36 *The Hunger* is a 1983 erotic horror film directed by Tony Scott.
37 In 1980, Bowie played the part, including on Broadway, without any cosmetic enhancements, using only his body to convey John Merrick's monstrosity.
38 While Ziggy and Aladdin Sane might be viewed as separate characters, and while Bowie emphasised Ziggy's cleaner lines in contrast to Aladdin Sane's ephemerality (Shaar Murray, 1973), in many ways Aladdin Sane is perhaps best viewed as "Ziggy goes to America," what David Buckley has described as "an English stylisation of American sounds, ideas and images" (Buckley, 2005, p. 156).
39 Girard, 1986; Bauman, 1993.
40 Derrida, 1995, pp. 386–387.
41 Canguilhem, 1964.
42 Foucault, 2003.
43 Derrida, 1995.
44 See, for example, Davidson, 1991, pp. 36–67; Cohen, 1996; Lykke and Braidotti, 1996; Graham, 2002; Shildrick, 2002.

45 Cohen, 1999, p. 22.
46 Critchley, 2014, pp. 54–55.
47 Cohen, 1996, p. 6.
48 Gregory, 2008; Bangs, 1976; MacDonald, 1973, 2013.
49 Critchley, 2014.
50 1972 (RCA).
51 1974 (RCA).
52 1995 (Arista/BMG/RCA (Europe) and Virgin (USA)).
53 The tour, which commenced on 2 February 1976 and launched the *Station to Station* album, which was released on 23 January 1976, was also referred to as the Thin White Duke tour and the White Light tour. It is not to be confused with Bowie's second Isolar tour in 1978.
54 Musician's Union, 1976; Jones, 1977.
55 There is an extensive literature on the concept of the sublime. In particular, see Edmund Burke (1998) and Immanuel Kant (2009). I am using the term here, and in the essays that follow, to mean an encounter with something lacking clear boundaries, something instilling a sense of awe, and something taking us beyond, outside ourselves.
56 Burroughs, 1985, p. 47.
57 Rae, 2019.
58 Lindsay, 2016.
59 Critchley, 2014, p. 144.
60 Beals, 2007. See also Badiou, 2012.
61 Badiou, 2012, p. 22.
62 Badiou, 2012, p. 28.
63 Foucault, 1988a, p. 154.

Difference

1

LAW'S MONSTERS

The hopeful undecidability of David Bowie

Introduction

In this essay, we consider the figure of the monster, a figure that has haunted human societies across culture and through time. Indeed, at least in the West, the monster has been a formal category of the law. It is evident in Roman legal texts, including Justinian's Code.[1] In the English context, the monster entered the common law through the mid-thirteenth century writings of Henry de Bracton and survived until at least the late-nineteenth century.[2] The monster is also a template within social theory through which attempts have been made to make sense of the production and regulation of outsiders, especially perhaps those most threatening to the social and legal order.[3] While the relationship between human and monster is not one of absolute difference, because as we will see, being at least part-human is a necessary condition of being a monster (at least the kind of monster with which this essay is concerned),[4] the figure of the monster remains the type of difference we imagine to be at the furthest remove from us. In this respect, among the multiplicity of outsider figures generated within law[5] and social theory,[6] the monster is of particular interest.

Here we will explore the figure of the monster through three French philosophers, Georges Canguilhem, Michel Foucault and Jacques Derrida. The selection of Canguilhem and Foucault is informed by the fact this essay, while recognising the psychoanalytical insight that we are all monsters, that is, divided from ourselves,[7] seeks to explain why only some individuals and/or groups are singled out in particular historical moments for monsterisation. As Zakiya Hanafi has noted, monsters are perhaps best approached as "an ideological cluster," that is, "as an entity constructed and represented within a social group."[8] In my view, the theories of Canguilhem and Foucault offer greater analytical precision and explanatory power in addressing this question of the specific monster than do other theories

DOI: 10.4324/9781003140429-3

that concern themselves with monsters. Derrida will highlight for us what Canguilhem and Foucault neglect, namely the hopefulness of monsters and, therefore, will give us reason to embrace them. Bowie's contribution will be to bring these ideas to life.

David Bowie has always been special, more than special, otherworldly. A starman, who came to deliver us from the emptiness, the dreariness, the heteronormative fetters of English suburban life. However, attempts, especially after his death, to canonise or deify him, are misplaced. Because he wasn't a saint or a God, not even a rock God (Gasp). He was so much more than that. He was that figure that haunts law, the monster and what a monster he was. And, it is monsters, not Gods, who point the way: artistically, ethically, spiritually. This essay is about three things: monsters, hope and David Bowie. Monsters, because the monster is the outsider template *par excellence*. Hope, because monsters are quintessentially hopeful. Bowie, because he is the hopeful monster writ large. Of all the figures within popular culture, few embody the monster quite like David Bowie. Monsters then will be our object, hope our reason and Bowie our guide and delight. The monster, and Bowie as monster, brings all manner of legal and other categorical distinctions to crisis. For the purposes of this essay, however, and through Bowie, we will journey through the territory of gender and sexuality in order to explore these themes. Before turning to Bowie, however, I will first present a framework for thinking about the structure of the monster.

A monster framework

In laying some theoretical ground, I will provide some examples of monsters that might have been covered in this essay as alternatives to Bowie, and some examples that ought not to be treated as monsters at all. In proceeding in this way, I aim to home in on the object of our inquiry, for not all scary creatures are monsters. In choosing examples, there are many directions one could take. Thus, we could have considered physical monsters of the past, ones that have preoccupied us since antiquity. This would be a story of how science has sought to kill off monsters, or at least, has tested our willingness to suspend our disbelief in them. Such a history would include consideration of the social and legal treatment of bestial humans, conjoined twins and hermaphrodites, three figures which, according to Foucault, preoccupied the West during the late Middle Ages, the Renaissance and the Classical period, respectively.[9]

Alternatively, we could focus on science as the creator, rather than the destroyer of monsters. One contemporary example that might be explored here is the creation of human/animal admixed embryos.[10] Or perhaps, we might venture beyond reality into the territory of fiction, that is, if to invoke the monster is not already to have made that journey. Thus, we might have considered werewolves, vampires, the creature in Frankenstein,[11] or perhaps Stevenson's *Jekyll and Hyde*[12] or Marvel Comics' the *Incredible Hulk*. In choosing these examples of fiction, I have deliberately avoided King Kong, Godzilla and Cookie Monster. The reason for such exclusions is that I want to distinguish between monsters, on the one hand, and beasts or creatures, on the other. In other words, a key thing about monsters is that they are part human.

Another type of figure I wish to exclude from the definition of monster includes examples like James Cameron's *The Terminator* (1984).[13] Such figures are excluded, despite being apparently human/non-human hybrids, because they are inorganic. As Canguilhem notes: "the qualification of monster must be reserved for organic beings."[14] There is, he insists, no such thing as "a mechanical monster."[15] Rather, the monster presupposes departure or deviation from some morphological norm. This can be thought of in terms of physical lack or, more often, excess. It is, therefore, at least for Canguilhem, a high degree of physical human difference that leads to a conclusion of *monstrosity*.

However, he does not equate mere monstrosity with the term monster, though such conflations abound in the monster literature. This is because, as Canguilhem stresses, the monster is a double-effect. Though it requires monstrosity, this proves to be a necessary rather than a sufficient condition of monster production. The other condition is *monstrousness*. By monstrousness, Canguilhem is referring to a body's relationship to the law. He is pointing to a requirement that a body contravene or transgress law. As he puts it, monstrosity and monstrousness "are a duality of concepts with the same etymological root" and are "at the service of two forms of normative judgment, the medical and the legal."[16] In other words, the monster is to be understood as the effect of a particular law/nature nexus. For Canguilhem, the monster is the effect of a breach of nature (understood as morphological irregularity) and a breach of law (understood as a crisis of classification).

Foucault understands the monster in similar terms. As he points out, it appears "only when [the] confusion [of nature] comes up against, overturns, or disturbs civil, canon or religious law."[17] Thus, for Foucault, like Canguilhem, the monster is not simply an outlaw. It not only refuses and escapes the law. It renders it unintelligible. In the face of the monster, Foucault notes, "[l]aw must either question its own foundations, or its practice, or fall silent, or abdicate, or appeal to another reference system."[18] However, unlike Canguilhem, Foucault reworks the idea of a breach of nature to take account of the historical shift in the regulatory preoccupations of the state from the body to the 'soul' or psyche.[19] This reworking is important because it enables the idea of the monster to extend beyond the physical body to include, a truly modern figure, the monster within. While Canguilhem took the view that the natural sciences had killed off monsters,[20] Foucault points to the social sciences as spawning, in the mid-to-late nineteenth century, a multiplicity of new, diluted "everyday monster[s],"[21] which he termed "abnormal individuals."[22]

It is then this idea of the monster, as a human/non-human hybrid, existing in nature but confounding law, that I want to take up. This is because it is this understanding of the monster, whether understood in terms of the body and/or the psyche, that produces in us the greatest anxiety. And what produces the greatest anxiety is the simultaneous distance and proximity we bear to monsters. In one sense, they prop us up through creating the fantasy of stable ground beneath our feet. They do so through providing an outside to our human outline. Yet, we can never keep them at arms-length. We are full of doubts. Wherever we draw the line, monsters, as Jeffrey Cohen has pointed out, highlight permeability.[23]

The hopefulness of monsters

Having made these preliminary remarks, and before proceeding to Bowie, I want to say something about hope, about the hopefulness of monsters. Foucault and Canguilhem provide us with a structure for understanding *how* monsters appear and why they fade away. They say little, if anything, however, about their hope-fulness, though Foucault perhaps alludes to their promise in his somewhat prob-lematic description of nineteenth-century hermaphrodite, Herculine Barbin's life as "a happy limbo of non-identity."[24] It might seem counter-intuitive to think of monsters as hopeful. After all, monsters, both of the flesh, as well as those within literature and popular culture, have often been imagined and portrayed as portents of dystopia, as figures that lie in wait over the horizon. Yet, they have also been viewed as hopeful signs. Certainly, the Latin word *monstrare*, meaning to show forth or demonstrate, rather than to warn,[25] placed the emphasis on hope. And after the fifth-century writings of Saint Augustine, monsters were read increasingly as signs of the power and glory of God to come.[26] In any event, monsters are intrinsically hopeful for at least two reasons.

First, they guarantee us a future. Second, and relatedly, they point to the place of the sacred in a world without God. Let me explain. In relation to ensuring a future, Derrida reminds us that:

> the future is necessarily monstrous: the figure of the future, that is, that which can only be surprising, that for which we are not prepared . . . is heralded by species of monsters. A future that would not be monstrous would not be a future; it would already be a predictable, calculable, and programmable tomorrow.[27]

In other words, the future is not simply a matter of temporality. It is not only time to come. Rather, it is time + surprise. Without the possibility of the wholly unexpected, there would be, could be, no future in Derrida's sense. Rather, an endless series of repetitive tomorrows would be our miserable lot. The future, both as that which we anticipate and that which we hope arrives, is necessarily the stuff of novelty or surprise. In this important sense, the monster prefigures the future. Turning to the place of the sacred, monsters point to it, and they do so irrespec-tive of whether they are considered good or bad, the sacred being indifferent to such moral distinctions.[28] Whatever else it might be, the sacred is that which holds value.[29] What gives something value, as Desmond Manderson notes, is "its inability to be adequately reduced to our own preexisting terms. Value is what is left over [when] our efforts to know, define, and to commodify"[30] have been exhausted. It is because monsters represent an excess of signification, of language itself, being simultaneously human and non-human, that they have value. It is precisely their irreducibility that speaks to each of us and to our collective parts. In contrast to commodification, they call for solidarity, connection and love. And so, we ought to embrace monsters. By embrace, I mean, not only the differences that mark others and lie within ourselves but also what the monster concept represents more broadly: change, ambiguity, instability, complexity, openness. Because we want a future, and because we want both to love and to be loved, embrace the monster we must.

Bowie as hopeful monster

As philosopher, Simon Critchley, has pointed out, Bowie's music "is a discord with the world that can allow a certain demundanization, a withdrawal that might permit us to see things in a utopian light."[31] In other words, there is something hopeful about David Bowie. And hope is something that connects him to the monster, though, as we shall see, it is not the only thing. More than any other figure within popular culture, Bowie captured the idea and promise of the monster. He did so not only through transgressive art and music but through imagining and creating exciting futures and because he pointed to the place of the sacred in a world without God. He is quite literally the daddy-o of late twentieth-century monsters of popular culture and the mother of others as well as those to come. Who better than Bowie to exemplify the monster? Bowie, a figure who, due to permanent anisocoria (a dilated pupil) in his left eye appeared to have eyes of different form and colour[32] and, therefore, had the appearance of being an outsider before he even got going and who would later play that role in film (an alien in Nicholas Roeg's *The Man Who Fell to Earth* 1976, a vampire in Tony Scott's *The Hunger* 1983), television (a degenerate in Bertolt Brecht's *Baal* on the BBC 1982) and theatre (*The Elephant Man* on Broadway 1980). Bowie, who had "always had a repulsive need to be something more than human."[33] So, with an eye to the promise of monsters, let us turn to this *outré* figure extraordinaire.

In the chorus to his 1980 song, 'Scary Monsters (And Super Creeps),'[34] Bowie, through the lyric 'keep me running, running scared,' alludes to at least three things that are central to thinking about monsters. One, monsters can scare the shit out of us and, two, we like it. Or, to put it another way, the monster is an amalgam of fear and desire. We look away, but we always look back. We are spellbound, transfixed. Or as Bowie puts it, we simply 'can't say no to the beauty and the beast.'[35] And the reason for this is that there is something tantalising about monsters. They are strange, awesome in fact, yet strangely familiar. This produces in us a sense of the uncanny (*unheimlich*).[36] Third, through the encounter, monsters, as Bowie says, keep us running, they urge us forward into the unknown. They call us to be greater than we are, to move beyond ourselves, our current predicament, our trivialities. In this sense, monsters, while perhaps terrifying, represent hope.

In other words, Bowie understood what is true in art as it is in life: stasis equals death. In refusing the tyranny of fixed identity, as well as the purity of genre, Bowie, like the monster he so eloquently symbolised and embodied, made possible, ushered in the new. However, Bowie aimed not merely to change. He was not simply a chameleon. Rather, he always sought to fuck things up. That is, he was not concerned only with motion but with challenging the taken-for-granted, the axiomatic, the self-evident. As he stated in 1998, "[o]nce something is categorised and accepted, it becomes part of the tyranny of the mainstream, and it loses all potency."[37] Like Foucault, he seemed to understand such an approach to be absolutely necessary as a ground-clearing exercise. No respecter of tradition, his *modus operandi* was perpetual reinvention or as Bowie himself has characterised it, perhaps with an emphasis on mischief: "hit and run."[38]

And in his creative endeavours, Bowie was monster-like, both in the sense of being incredibly prolific (gargantuan)[39] and in his promiscuity (his mixing of genres).[40] Indeed, Bowie's originality lies precisely in this practice. He embraced derivation. Or we might say, he liked to borrow, or perhaps, given the distinction between talent and genius,[41] steal. He liked to steal and he liked to mix. In the face of musical and other artistic genres, Bowie was incapable of fidelity. In terms of music, he flirted with folk and the whimsy of English musical hall (think Anthony Newley and Lionel Bart),[42] then looked to Black America (rock 'n' roll/soul/funk), before turning to the minimalism and discordant notes of Krautrock. The Berlin years[43] ended with the album, *Lodger* – Bowie could never stick around for long. In terms of imagery, he moved through mod, hippy, a period as a mime, androgynous space invader, amoral aristocrat, clown and so forth. In relation to gender and sexuality, Bowie's playfulness shone a light on their contingency.

Bowie and gender/sexual ambiguity

Historically, the monster label has been attached to bodies that defied the social and legal order, especially those viewed as problematising gender (man/woman) or species (human/animal)[44] distinctions. In terms of challenge to the gender order, the figure of the hermaphrodite has preoccupied us since antiquity. Moreover, our preoccupation with this particular figure has, if anything, intensified over time. Thus, Foucault has argued that hermaphrodites (individuals who we today refer to as intersex) were the "privileged monsters" of the eighteenth century,[45] by which he means anxiety surrounding them reached its climax during this historical period. By the century's end, however, the hermaphrodite, and the third gender problematic they presented, had been corralled, demystified, as medical science reimagined sex in binary terms.[46] However, while science attempts to kill off monsters, that is, to explain them away, to incorporate them within some comforting order, monsters, as we know, *always* return.

And as noted earlier, they did so through the sexological and psychiatric lexicon of 'abnormality.'[47] In this regard, monstrosity became less an effect of the legal and cultural reading of bodies, in terms of their physical parts, and more an effect of their gender performances and sexual desires. That is, the 'problem' became one of deviant sexuality and gender performances through which it was rendered 'evident.' It is in this context of monstrosity having been turned outside-in that we turn to Bowie. From the outset, he struck an androgynous pose. On the original *The Man Who Sold the World* album cover,[48] we see Bowie reclining on a *chaise longue*, in full pre-Raphaelite transvestic splendour. On *Hunky Dory*,[49] we see his likeness to Dietrich, or perhaps Greta Garbo.[50] With the arrival of Ziggy[51] and Aladdin Sane, his androgyny morphed into more highly sexualised camp. Think 'Jean Genie' or Jean Genet.[52] Bowie's gender undecidability can be contrasted with "the prevailing masculinist subculture that dominated British Rock in the mid to late 1960s."[53] While Ziggy played guitar, Bowie rarely did.[54] In opposition to the *Cock Rock*[55] of the period, and the compulsory heterosexuality to which it spoke,[56] Bowie inserted the feminine but not in a shy way. Through fakery, he highlighted the artificiality of rock[57] but also the constructedness of gender.[58] Moreover, Bowie's gender ambiguity was not confined to movement of his physical body, his animal grace, or to his playfulness with the cultural insignia of gender. He also expressed the multiplicity of gender through his voice, often within a single song, what Shelton Waldrep has referred to as an operatic approach.[59] Examples of this technique include his shift from a deep baritone to a soaring falsetto on 'Golden Years' ('Don't let me hear you say'/'Angel') and, perhaps at his most sublime, on 'Sweet Thing' ('It's safe in the city'/'Will you see').[60]

In relation to sexuality, and at a time when homophobia remained pervasive in the US and the UK, Bowie, though married to Angie, came out as gay,[61] the first really major star to just come right out and say it.[62] Later he repositioned as bi, then as a "closet heterosexual."[63] Moreover, during his travels across the hetero-homo divide, and perhaps beyond it, Bowie's sexual object choices transcended cis-sexuality.[64] That is, during his Berlin period, he had a lengthy relationship with muse and famous transgender cabaret star, Romy Haag.[65] Ultimately, when asked the sexual identity question, Bowie expressed only boredom. Yawn. Moreover, he openly shunned gay politics. He did not want to lead a movement. As Michael Watts has noted: Bowie "despise[d] . . . tribal qualities."[66] In this respect, he was more like Oscar Wilde than Andre Gide.[67] That is, more queer, than gay or bi, or not. Exactly. As with his approach to gender, Bowie's refusal to adopt a fixed sexual identity produces a crisis of classification. In contrast to the relatively muted threat posed by homosexuality, which, after all, serves to bolster heterosexuality as 'abnormal' mirror image, a queer sensibility throws the cat among the pigeons. In Foucault's terms, Bowie's fleshy and interior sexual monstrosity align with monstrousness.

In terms of Bowie's sexual playfulness, we can situate him on both sides of Noel Carroll's distinction for conceptualising monsters, namely *fusion* and *fisson*.[68] Fusion refers to mixture in point of time, whereas fisson refers to the occupation of the body by different entities at different times. Thus, we might contrast the mythic figure of the *Minotaur*[69] (fusion) with *Jekyll and Hyde* or the *Incredible Hulk* (fisson). However, drawing on Foucault, and thereby shifting the focus from the body to the 'soul' or psyche, we might recognise Bowie's bisexual *fusion* while at the same time recognising fisson, that is, his apparent shifts from straight to gay and gay to straight. Ultimately, Bowie eludes the distinction, refusing to take a position in a move that is both queer and pre-queer. After all, the faker was always much too fast to take that test.

Conclusion

To conclude, Bowie, both in flesh and as a series of artistic and musical representations, can be viewed as occupying, nay celebrating, the position of the monster. In contrast to the certainty of Law, he offers undecidability, ambiguity, hybridity, impurity, metamorphosis. In relation to nature, he introduces and celebrates physical and psychic irregularity. He is a creature both of and for our postmodern age, embracing "the destruction and rearticulation of the human in the name of [something] more capacious."[70] In preference to the default position of "all too human"[71] the monster, and Bowie as monster, provides a bridge between where we are now and where or who we would like to be. So, let us embrace monsters, so much better than Gods, with 'their tragic endless lives.'[72] Not Gods who lay down the law, but monsters who laugh at its hubris. Not Gods, dreary tomorrows without end, but monsters and the exciting futures they herald.

I remember when Elvis died. It was kind of sad, but I didn't cry. It was the same with John Lennon three years later and countless others since. But, on 10 January 2016, I did cry. I cried quite a lot. Partly because Bowie was the soundtrack to much of my life, especially my youth. But to foreground nostalgia would be to misrepresent the experience and its temporality. For in mourning Bowie's passing the sense of loss is palpable, as it must be when a true monster dies. What we feel, we who are not heathen,[73] is not nostalgia for the past, but rather what Bowie has described as "future nostalgia,"[74] that is, a nostalgia for things that didn't happen, but still might or, as he explains elsewhere, for a future that we have already seen, perhaps one that keeps returning, hovering on the horizon.[75] In other words, nostalgia for Bowie speaks to hope, not sentimentality. It points to our deep longing for connection, for love, for an experience of the sacred in the here and now and in the future.

And yet, even in death, something Bowie styled as he had life, he left us with hope, a parting caress. I refer here to his final album and requiem, *Blackstar*, released only two days before his death and which instantly went viral.[76] Through the song 'Lazarus,' Bowie points to resurrection, to a return.[77] Of course, there will be no more Bowie, other than in celluloid and forever. But there will be other hopeful monsters. How could it be otherwise? A life without monsters would be unimaginable and unbearable.

Notes

1 It is referred to in the writings of Paulus (Digest 1.5.14), Ulpian (Digest 50.16.38; D. 50.16.135) and Justinian (Code 6.29.3) (see Nicholas and Metzger, 1976).

2 The figure of the monster first appeared in the mid-thirteenth century common law writings of Henry de Bracton (1968, vol 2, pp. 51, 308–309, vol 4, p. 209) and reappeared in various subsequent legal commentaries, most notably those of Edward Coke (1979) and William Blackstone (1979, vol 1, pp. 292–294). For more detail concerning these and other English legal texts referring to monsters, see Sharpe, 2010, 2017.

3 See, for example, Davidson, 1991, pp. 36–67; Cohen, 1996; Lykke and Braidotti, 1996; Graham, 2002; Shildrick, 2002.

4 Non-human hybrids such as Pegasus or the Griffin might also be viewed as monsters. In Greek mythology, Pegasus is a horse with the wings of a bird. The Griffin is a mythical creature possessing the body, tail and rear legs of a lion and the head and wings of an eagle. However, this essay focuses on human/non-human hybrids because it is these kinds of monsters that induce in us the greatest anxiety.

5 Outsider figures emerging within law include the leper, the idiot, the lunatic, and the deformed or disabled (for further discussion see Sharpe, 2010, pp. 22–24).

6 Other well-known templates generated within social theory include the *scapegoat* (Girard, 1986) and the *stranger* (Bauman, 1993). For a discussion of the advantages the monster offers over these templates see Sharpe, 2010, pp. 24–29.

7 Cohen, 1996.

8 Hanafi, 2000, p. 14.

9 Foucault, 2003, p. 66.

10 Some jurisdictions allow the creation of human/animal admixed embryos for non-reproductive research purposes. For example, s. 4A(4) Human Fertilisation and Embryology Act 2008 (UK).

11 Shelley, 2010.

12 Stevenson, 1986.

13 Terminators are androids, rather than cyborgs. While they have living tissue, they are not living organisms with robotic body parts.

14 Canguilhem, 1964, p. 28.

15 Canguilhem, 1964, p. 28.

16 Canguilhem, 1964, p. 30.

17 Foucault, 2003, p. 63.

18 Foucault, 2003, p. 64.

19 Foucault, 1977. Accordingly, Foucault does not insist on a causal relationship between monstrosity and monstrousness. Conversely, Canguilhem views the former term as an effect of the latter, that is, a result of "an animal's carnival" (1964, pp. 30–31).

20 Canguilhem, 1964, p. 38.

21 Foucault, 2003, p. 57.

22 Foucault, 2003, p. 57. The monster is a key figure within Foucault's genealogy of the abnormal individual.

23 Cohen, 1996, p. 6.

24 Foucault, 1980a, Introduction xiii.

25 Epstein, 1995, p. 19.

26 Daston, 1991, p. 95.

27 Derrida, 1995, pp. 386–387.

28 (Durkheim, 1965a, 1965b). Durkheim does not equate the sacred with the divine.

29 Indeed, anything we consider inherently valuable might be a candidate, including 'some supreme principle of life such as love, freedom, equality or justice' (Anttonen, 2000, p. 281).

30 Manderson, 2006, p. 138.

31 Critchley, 2014, pp. 38–39.

32 Hunt, 2015, pp. 175–195.

33 Crowe, 1976a.

34 *Scary Monsters* album, 1980 RCA.

35 'Beauty and the Beast' (*Heroes* album, 1977 RCA).

36 Freud, 2003.

37 Kimmelman, 1998.

38 MTV Interview, 1995.

39 Bowie produced 27 studio albums, numerous live albums, as well as a body of films, theatre work and art.

40 Bowie has described himself as "aesthetically promiscuous" (MTV Interview, 1995).

41 The quote "talent borrows, genius steals" is often attributed to Oscar Wilde, though he may well have stolen it from somebody else. In relation to Bowie, see Trynka, 2011, pp. 1–4.

42 Anthony Newley was an actor, singer and songwriter. Lionel Bart was a writer and composer of pop music and musicals, most notably, *Oliver* in 1960.

43 During this period (1977–1979), Bowie was influenced by a number of German bands including the android-like Kraftwerk and Neu.

44 Thomas, 1983; Salisbury, 1994; Fudge, 2000. We will explore this theme in the final essay in the collection.

45 Foucault, 2003, p. 66.

46 As Thomas Laqueur has explained, prior to the eighteenth century, and since the time of Galen of Pergamum (c. 210 AD) the body was understood in terms of a one-sex model whereby men and women were considered to be two forms of one essential sex. By the nineteenth century, medical science insisted that "[a]ny notion of genuine sexual ambiguity or neutrality is nonsense because sex is absolutely there in and throughout the body" (Laqueur, 1990, p. 136).

47 Foucault, 2003, p. 57.

48 1970 Mercury.

49 1971 (RCA).

50 Pegg, 2002, p. 232.

51 *The Rise and Fall of Ziggy Stardust and the Spiders from Mars* album, 1972 RCA.

52 'Jean Genie' was released as a single in 1972, and subsequently on the *Aladdin Sane* album, 1973 RCA. The title of the song is an allusion to Jean Genet, the famous French novelist and playwright. Many of his novels deal with themes of transgressive homosexuality.

53 Peraino, 2012, p. 154.

54 Peraino, 2012, p. 157.

55 *Cock Rock* is a genre of rock music, which commenced in the late 1960s. It emphasises an aggressive form of male sexuality (Frith, 1981, p. 227).

56 Rich, 1980.

57 As Ken McLeod notes, "Bowie's conscious construction of an alien rock star was certainly meant to shed light on the artificiality of rock in general" (2003, p. 341). See also Philip Auslander, 2006, p. 106.

58 Butler, 1993.

59 Waldrep, 2015, p. 106.

60 On the *Station to Station* (1976) and *Diamond Dogs* (1974) albums respectively (both RCA). See O'Leary, 2010a.

61 Watts, 1972.

62 Savage, 1980.

63 Oppenheim, 2016. Bowie's assertion of a straight identity during the HIV/AIDS crisis was experienced by some within the gay community as a betrayal (Brooker, 2017, Chp 5).

64 *Cissexual* is a term coined by Julia Serano, 2007, Chp 8. It refers to people whose gender identities align with their birth designated sex.

65 Kohn, 2016.

66 Watts, 1972. In a 1977 interview Bowie stated: "I can't stand sets of people in any way, shape or form; politically, artistically or socially, a set of people has the most devastating effect on one's chances of producing anything" (Shaar Murray, 1977).

67 Dollimore, 1987.

68 Carroll, 1990, p. 47.

69 The Minotaur is a creature from Greek mythology possessing a bull's head and a man's body.
70 Butler, 2004, p. 35.
71 Nietzsche, 1994.
72 'The Supermen' (*The Man Who Sold the World* album, 1970 Mercury).
73 'Heathen' (*Heathen* album, 2002 ISO/Columbia). Bowie's *Heathen* will be discussed in the final essay which deals with the theme of love.
74 Quoted by Shelton Waldrep, 2015, p. 2.
75 MacKinnon, 1980, p. 37.
76 2016 ISO/Columbia/Sony.
77 Though whether a 'return' is desired is much more ambiguous, as Critchley notes in referring to the Biblical story of Lazarus: "[n]obody asked Lazarus if he actually wanted to come back from the grave and he does not seem particularly happy to be back. . . . Maybe Lazarus isn't so much the story of a heroic resurrection that proves Jesus's messianic credentials, but a sad tale of someone being pulled back to life without really wanting it at all" (Critchley, 2014, pp. 192–193).

Authenticity

2

AUTHENTICITY

What a drag!

Introduction

This essay considers the idea of *authenticity* through the vehicle of David Bowie. It may seem odd to select Bowie for this purpose. After all, he has been repeatedly accused of inauthenticity. Thus, Keith Richards has said of Bowie, "it's all pose. It's all fucking posing."[1] And in an ever so slightly less acerbic assessment, famous music critic, Lester Bangs, expressed disappointment and frustration with Bowie, because of what he saw as Bowie's eclecticism, kleptomania, shamelessness and pretension, the fact Bowie "had showbiz written all over him."[2] Other music critics have lined up to join "the Bowie execution [goon] squad."[3] Thus, we learn Bowie's records are "all style" with "no meaning at all,"[4] that he "compromised with showbiz, with the whole manipulative process of image and stardom,"[5] and that he is the epitome of "shallowness, charlatanism [and] affectation,"[6] "a dilettante, a style vampire who had his finger on the pulse but never his hand on his heart."[7] Even the great John Martyn, who gave Nick Drake[8] a run for his money, declared Bowie "a poseur. I don't think he's lived a quarter of the things he sings about and, to me, living it is crucial."[9] The point Martyn insisted, metaphorically speaking, is "to be able to take [your] clothes off in front of everybody."[10] This image of Bowie as inauthentic, as false, a phoney, perhaps reached its most dramatic moment at the time of John Lennon's assassination. Apparently, the Holden Caulfield[11] obsessed Mark Chapman had listed Bowie second on his hit list and had booked a front-row seat to see Bowie's performance of the *Elephant Man* on Broadway the following night.[12] Or, then again, perhaps it was later, much later, though again in New York, at the time of the great Nat Tate art world hoax.[13]

This view of Bowie as inauthentic couples authenticity with truth. This nexus continues to hold sway over the collective mindset and explains why some artists and critics have damned Bowie and viewed his artistic project as trivial. As

DOI: 10.4324/9781003140429-5

Richard Middleton notes, music culture at large continues to invest in this idea of authenticity as being of "critical primacy."[14] Indeed, and commenting on musical performance, Peter Kivy claims it continues to signify "[t]he highest praise one can bestow."[15] However, this essay will argue, following philosopher Simon Critchley, that "Bowie's genius [lies in] allow[ing] us to break the superficial link that seems to connect" authenticity with truth.[16] Thus, the essay will not attempt to defend Bowie against accusations of inauthenticity, albeit, as we will see, a case can be made for doing so, at least in some respects. To mount a defence of this kind would be to miss the point. After all, in the face of such accusations Bowie, who often referred to himself in the third person,[17] simply shrugged. Not because they were ridiculous or untrue but because inauthenticity was something he embraced to powerful artistic effect. As he stated, "I have always engaged in the idea of an entertainer who performs authenticity . . . one cannot be authentic."[18]

This approach led music critic, Jon Savage, to describe Bowie as the first postmodern rock star.[19] Indeed, Bowie has described himself as a representative of "an embryonic form of postmodernism"[20] and as "responsible for a whole new school of pretensions."[21] Thus, Bowie was supremely aware of his inauthenticity. More than aware, he owned it. And crucially, for our purposes, he insisted, rightly in my view, that "[a]s an artist of artifice [he had] more integrity than any one of [his] contemporaries."[22] In other words, as Critchley argues, Bowie understood that authenticity and truth are not synonymous terms and he contributed significantly to wider appreciation of this reality. While Bowie often made tongue-in-cheek and off-the-cuff remarks, his claim of integrity should be taken not only literally, but seriously. The central claim of this essay then is that Bowie's work is truthful as opposed to authentic, deeply meaningful rather than a matter of provenance. Indeed, understanding these distinctions is essential to understanding Bowie and the sublime quality of much of his work. In making this case, it is first necessary to provide an analysis of the concept of authenticity before proceeding to consider how Bowie subverted it, or at least particular understandings of it.

On authenticity

In the modern sense, the idea of authenticity is traceable, as Lionel Trilling notes, to a series of important cultural changes in the seventeenth and eighteenth centuries, whereby understandings of what it means to be human became associated with individual uniqueness or distinctiveness, irrespective of the demands of social norms.[23] In short, 'sincere man,' Hegel's "[hero] of dumb service"[24] was superseded by 'authentic man.' This shift, which found philosophical[25] and literary[26] expression through romanticism,[27] was associated with the rise of market liberalism and increasing awareness of its ideological effects. In the face of disenchantment of the world and alienation of the self, ushered in by capitalism, older moral distinctions – right/wrong, good/bad, virtue/viciousness – were replaced, or at least supplemented, by a new dyad: real/fake. In other words, concern over authenticity reflected a growing sense that the truth of one's nature had been masked by economic forces and the social and cultural norms and expectations one had inter-nalised. According to Charles Taylor, this led to increasing awareness of what he has referred to as "internal space," or inner life,[28] something that emerged as separate from one's public self.[29]

The idea of authenticity then, and certainly the idea of authentic selfhood, is associated with the practice of being true to oneself. In terms of art and music specifically, we might think about authenticity in terms of an autobiographical rela-tionship between artist and artwork. Thus, we might ask, does the artist communi-cate something truthful about herself through her artwork? That is, is her artwork personal testimony or confession, a turning of inside out, or is it 'merely' enter-tainment designed to please an audience? Or we might shift our attention to the authenticity of performance[30] and ask whether an artist bears her 'soul' emotion-ally? As Peter Kivy has noted, this type of performance authenticity involves being true to one's 'artistic self' rather than an historical tradition.[31] The idea of musical authenticity has also been associated with ideas of autonomy, an uncompromising attitude, non-conformity, a back to basics approach, a DIY ethos and a refusal to 'sell out,'[32] that is, a refusal to allow commerce to trump art.[33] Some combination of this set of ideas can be seen to run through a series of musical forms, including jazz, folk, blues, rock 'n' roll, rock, punk, grunge and hip hop.[34] In particular, not selling out is such a powerful refrain within rock culture that it has, as Deena Weinstein notes, become part of its mythic structure.[35] After all, in the eyes of many music critics and fans, authenticity in rock was/is "founded upon its socially oppositional status."[36]

David Phillips has noted, "the word 'authentic' is one of an overlapping set of evaluations that includes sincere, true, honest, absolute, basic, essential, genuine, ideal, natural, original, perfect, pure, real, and right."[37] In other words, authenticity is only one means of assessing individuals and their works, while at the same time there appears to be some degree of slippage between authenticity and these other evaluative terms, and as Critchley notes, perhaps especially between authenticity and truth. Although Bowie is clearly not authentic in the sense of being absolute, ideal, natural, perfect or pure, and while he might be viewed as having sold out artistically during the 1980s (sorry), it could be argued that his work, taken as a whole, is authentic in the sense of being original and true, a point to which we shall return. However, as already noted, I do not intend to make a case for Bowie's authenticity, especially as Bowie himself eschewed the term. Rather, what should be recognised is that Bowie embodied some of the ideas to which Phillips refers. Crucially, this essay will argue there is something fundamentally more truthful about his music and art than many of his creative contemporaries and successors. It is to explaining and justifying this claim that attention now turns.

Subverting (artistic) authenticity

David Bowie challenged the notion of authenticity, its claim to authority,[38] its hotline to truth. Michel Foucault's insistence, "do not ask me who I am, and do not ask me to remain the same,"[39] might be read as a kind of Bowie manifesto. Foucault argued that we have falsely come to believe the 'truth' of the modern subject lies "lodgèd in our most secret nature" and "demands only to surface."[40] Bowie set himself against this idea of a core self, something unchanging, something that has always been there/us, something which requires articulation. He seemed to grasp the need for and lived out artistically, what Foucault has described as "an unending becoming."[41] That is, he saw himself, much like Oscar Wilde, as his own self-creation, a work of art. Moreover, while he steadfastly refused to bear his 'soul' ("Don't expect to find the real me . . . the David Jones . . . underneath all this"),[42] he introduced to a much wider audience the idea that "performing the 'other'" could be understood as your "authentic [or given the distinction already made, truthful] self."[43] That is, while John Martyn and other musicians sought to express truth as authenticity through getting their metaphorical kits off, Bowie preferred layers, cultural accoutrements.

While Bowie found the demands of authenticity, understood as referring to some kind of deep self to be a bore, he remains one of the most truthful artists precisely because he grasped, what Critchley has described as the 'truth of inauthenticity.'[44] Further, in terms of Taylor's distinction between inner life and the public self, Bowie, though perhaps likely to be seen by Taylor and others as superficial on account of his celebration of artifice,[45] emerges as a public self (or selves). Indeed, through emphasising surface over depth ('Andy Warhol, silver screen, can't tell them apart at all'),[46] Bowie laid ground for establishing communal bonds with his audience. He did so precisely because, unlike many singer–songwriters of his generation and since, he refused to penetrate audiences with his truth. Rather, through self-consciously donning masks, he sought to create spaces in which audience members could create and express their own truths. That is, Bowie encouraged more active forms of audience engagement and creative dialogue. After all, he saw himself as offering no message ("I have no message whatsoever. I really have nothing to say, no suggestions or advice, nothing").[47] Rather, he was the message.[48]

Through his music and performance, he shone a light on what is artificial in rock and the wider culture. He did so through an explicit strategy of fabrication and through letting audiences see the seams of fabricated things. In doing so, he enabled us to "escape from being riveted to the fact of who we are."[49] As George Reisch has noted, "Bowie wanted to subvert the idea of *artistic authenticity* that grew up around denim and flower power,"[50] though in the process be subverted much more, including for example, and as we saw in the first essay, ideas of gender and sexuality. As Douglas Rossinow has observed, the politics of the 1960s involved "a search for authenticity."[51] This carried over into music and broader youth culture. Indeed, it was already present in folk music, which, of course, is from where Dylan's musical earnestness, his embodiment of the spirit of Woody Guthrie, sprang.[52] Singer–songwriters like Dylan, Neil Young and Joni Mitchell expressed, or were widely regarded as expressing, "values of authenticity, depth, reality, immediacy and unity."[53]

While immediacy was important to Bowie,[54] he distanced himself from these other values, and from what he described as the "presumptuousness of the song-writer,"[55] preferring artifice, surface, fragmentation, imagination. Indeed, we might think of Bowie through the lens of situationism, as engaged in *detournement*,[56] as "subverting the spectacular function of celebrity."[57] Certainly, we might contrast the innocence of the self-styled authentic rock star with Bowie's knowingness. While not losing sight of the distinction already drawn between authenticity and truth, Bowie might be described as "authentically inauthentic,"[58] as revealing authenticity to be "no more authentic than any other self-consciously created identity."[59] In other words, Bowie recognised authenticity to be "ascribed, not inscribed."[60] Indeed, perhaps more than any other rock star, Bowie appeared wide-eyed, recognising his place "within a symbol-making process."[61]

Moreover, Bowie not only positioned himself against the idea of authenticity on artistic grounds. It was not simply that he was a child of Andy Warhol and William Burroughs. Rather, he also had serious misgivings concerning the hippie project and collective dreams or political utopias more generally. While Bowie immersed himself in the sentiments of the time, after all, he was only twenty during the Summer of Love, his relationship to hippie culture was more flirtation, he was never really of it. He 'never got it off on that revolution stuff, what a drag.'[62] Indeed, he had an ambivalent, if not cynical, relationship to hippie culture, to what might be described as a cult of authenticity, something he captured scathingly on the song, 'Cygnet Committee,'[63] its prescient lyrics anticipating John Lennon's announcement just a year later that 'the dream is over.'[64]

> And I open my eyes to look around,
> And I see a child laid slain on the ground,
> As a love machine lumbers through desolation rows,
> Ploughing down man, woman, listening to its command,
> But not hearing anymore,
> Not hearing anymore.

For the hippies, true expression of authenticity lay in individualism,[65] in introspective searching, what Charles Taylor and Christopher Lasch might describe as narcissistic naval-gazing.[66] Bowie, by contrast, seemed to grasp that "[t]here is no internal, psychic life that is not somehow staged by culture."[67] As he explained to Janine, 'But if you take an axe to me, You'll kill another man, Not me at all.'[68] In other words, being authentic is hard because authenticity is an illusion. Or as Bowie puts it: 'It's so hard for us to really be, Really you, And really me.'[69] In the face of this reality, he sought to pare back the self,[70] preferring to look out onto the world, to let it constitute him, and through him, through an artistic engagement with it, he revealed truth.

The authenticity-truth nexus, against which Bowie railed, also privileges a specific and circumscribed idea of originality, one that sets itself against imitation and derivation.[71] Yet, as James Curcio points out, "[t]rue originality would be a form of madness."[72] As Will Brooker notes, drawing on Roland Barthes,[73] "everything has been done before."[74] All that remains is to select, to mix and to play with the multiplicity of existing art objects and other cultural things. And, of course, Bowie is highly original in this sense. He embraced derivation, larceny, a refusal to honour genre and a willingness to act with infidelity. As he pointed out, "[a]ll art is unstable. Its meaning is not necessarily that implied by the author. There is no authoritative voice, there are only multiple readings."[75] His recognition, nay celebration, of such postmodern insights encouraged him to create readerly texts, ones that empowered listeners, rather than treating them as passive.

Bowie increasingly saw himself as a canvas on which to paint, creating as many meanings as fans could discern. As he stated in 1995, "the strength of my work" rests on there being "as much room for multi-interpretation as possible."[76] Indeed, he was more than happy to recognise, and sometimes adopt,[77] fans' interpretations of his lyrics. Moreover, and citing Marcel Duchamp,[78] he insisted, a work "is not finished until the audience come to it and add their own interpretation."[79] Like Barthes, he grasped the fact that "a text's unity lies not in its origin but its destination,"[80] or as Brooker has put it, it lies "not in the writer, but in us."[81] What mattered to Bowie was not static meaning, if that were possible, but rather drawing fans into an artistic, and at times avant-garde realm, one characterised by the random, by allusion,[82] and the more general play of signifiers, and by music both melodious and cacophonous. For it is here that truths about ourselves and our world are experienced, are felt.

In exploring these truths, we could explore many themes within Bowie's corpus. Here we will consider two: the personas, through which the studied faker encountered the world, and the lyrical and musical dissonance that lies at the heart of some of his best songs. In both contexts, we will see the truth of inauthenticity come through. In essence, Bowie imparts some important art/life lessons. And as Critchley has observed, the filthiest lesson Bowie's (all good) art imparts is that inauthenticity goes "all the way down, a series of repetitions and reenactments: fakes that strip away the illusion of reality in which we live and confront us with the reality of illusion."[83] This is, of course, how Bowie viewed hippie authenticity, his throw-away line, 'what a drag,' operating as a double entendre meaning both 'bore' and 'confection.'

Turning to Bowie's characters, his artistic presentations, his developing aesthetic and pausing only to note Bowie was himself a fiction destined to become more real than his creator,[84] he exchanged the alien messiah and proto-punk Ziggy[85] for the paranoid, corrupted and ephemeral Aladdin Sane,[86] only to morph into Halloween Jack, a dystopian figure who ushered in the year of the *Diamond Dogs*,[87] who in turn succumbed to the plastic soul-boy of *Young Americans*,[88] only to be sacrificed on the slab of the emotionally distant Thin White Duke,[89] an *Übermensch*[90] character who gestured aesthetically toward German modernism and the avant-garde, and finally to Pierrot, the tragi-comic fool-clown of *Scary monsters*.[91] In other words, throughout the 1970s, and with corpses piling up behind him, Bowie's dance went on and on. Moreover, because Bowie sought to privilege surface over depth, truth over authenticity, exchanging masks proved necessary because the mask, as Ericson Saint Clair points out, "ceases to be useful when it comes to be considered something more serious than simply a mask,"[92] a problem that can, and likely will, arise if a character is lived out too long.

Each of these characters provided Bowie with a perspective onto the world. In seeing the world through his characters, and through drawing on a multiplicity of cultural and musical reference points in putting them together – their look, their sound, their sensibility – Bowie effectively placed himself in the position of the 'other.' Thus, in constructing Ziggy, he drew, in true bricolage fashion, on a diverse range of cultural phenomenon, including Japanese Kabuki theatre costumes, mime, Stanley Kubrick's *Clockwork Orange* and its Droogs,[93] the Legendary Stardust Cowboy,[94] Judy Garland, fringe New York music (aka the Velvet Underground), androgyny and science fiction. With the Thin White Duke, he drew on Thomas Jerome Newton, the extraterrestrial character he played in Nicholas Roeg's film, *The Man Who Fell to Earth*, and on German expressionism, an aristocratic sensibility and a totalitarian, fascist mindset,[95] as well as on soul music and Krautrock. We need to remember here that Bowie was essentially an actor, a debt he owed, at least in part, to Lindsay Kemp.[96] That is, "he understood his own performing and his relationship to his audience in actorly terms."[97]

Moreover, and while perhaps not Marlon Brando, James Dean or Dustin Hoffman, Bowie was a method actor. He did not simply play a role for the duration of a show. Rather, his preparation and emotional investment in his characters were significant. Thus, as Ziggy or the Thin White Duke, he was interviewed as and lived as these characters for their duration. As Bowie later reflected, "Ziggy was a full-time job, twenty-four/seven."[98] and elsewhere, "It's no longer an act; I am him."[99] Fans, interviewers and others responded to him as Ziggy or the Duke. Bowie became these characters and saw the world through their eyes. These experiences of otherness, of different perspectives, of different emotions, enriched Bowie's work and enabled him to convey truths at odds with those of more pedestrian rock stars. Indeed, as Bowie explained, "[w]hen I don't have a character to play with, I stand in total ignorance of what's happening around me."[100] Through his characters, and, therefore, at a critical distance, Bowie soaked up and re-presented the world.

Turning to his songs, Bowie seemed able to trigger a sense of yearning. That is, through his "highly referential,"[101] though often cryptic lyrics, and his eclectic music he seemed to point to something beyond, to some palpable truth behind the appearance of things. And while Bowie "moved relentlessly from illusion to illusion,"[102] he always seemed to get closer to "a felt, corporeal truth"[103] than those who accused him of fakery. We might say, fans recognised themselves or at least their possible future selves, in the gaps that peppered Bowie's words, sounds and visions, in the spaces between melody and cacophony. Rather than unity or wholeness, he offered the truth of fragments. For a particularly dramatic example of this, listen to the triptych of songs, 'Sweet Thing/Candidate/Sweet Thing (Reprise),' which conjure up a set of affecting images.[104] Bowie's fragments have special resonance, dealing as they do with isolation, abandonment, fear and anxiety, what

Bowie has described as "all of the [emotional] high points of one's life."[105] They just feel so right. While Bowie maintained a certain intellectual distance from his work, and while some of his characters, most notably the Thin White Duke, were emotionally cut off, much of his work is deeply emotional, affecting. That is, it bears the hallmarks of truth. And this affect was produced by a kind of playfulness, one that had no truck with staying in lane, with genre, with authenticity. Rather, Bowie offered shifting moods, a remarkably subtle and versatile voice,[106] cut-up lyrics,[107] infidelity to each and every musical style, a preference to show rather than tell, and always, always surprise.

Conclusion

This essay has considered the idea of authenticity, an idea that in cultural terms has operated as a synonym for artistic and other truth. This idea is perhaps best captured by the figure of the singer-songwriter whose work is understood as biography or confession, a turning of inside out. In the face of this authenticity-truth nexus, the essay drew on Bowie to argue not only does truth not depend on authenticity but in the most important sense truth is best understood and experienced as inauthenticity. It is Bowie's self-conscious and unapologetic subversion of (artistic) authenticity and his embracing of the reality of inauthenticity through his art that marks him out, not as a phoney but as a truth-teller.

While Bowie's many critics looked to him, to his many poses, to prop up the idea of the authentic rock star, the contrast serves a quite different purpose, namely, to highlight the constructed nature of rock and the derivative nature of art. Ultimately, the difference between Bowie and his detractors, such as Keith Richards or John Martyn, lies not in Bowie's artifice and their 'realness' but in their innocence and Bowie's knowingness concerning the grand illusion that is authenticity. In the face of this illusion, Bowie charted a protean path, recreating himself in dialogue with the world and everything it offers. Moreover, and importantly, through abdicating authority over his work, through creating readerly texts, he helped constitute fans as active agents and creative communities. In doing so, he enabled his work to speak to experiences of personal truth "in all of [their] chaotic complexity."[108]

Notes

1 Gregory, 2008. Charlie Watts has also been critical of Bowie (Morgan Britton, 2018). It is interesting that some members of the Rolling Stones, in particular, have been so critical of Bowie's contribution to the rock 'n' roll canon, given that since the early 1970s the Stones effectively became their own tribute band. After Bowie's death, Richards stated: "David was a true original in everything he did" (Goodman, 2016), though we should perhaps read this concession in relation to protocols that operate when speaking of the dead.
2 Bangs, 1976.
3 MacDonald, 1973.
4 Andrew Weiner quoted in MacDonald, 1973.
5 Dave Laing, 1973, quoted in Buckley, 2005, p. 104.

6 Richard Williams quoted in MacDonald, 1973. Other rock music critics have criticised Bowie for what they saw as his "incipient elitism" and "pretensions to art and intellect" (Hebdige, 1995, p. 60).
7 Pegg, 2002, p. 1.
8 Humphries, 1998.
9 MacDonald, 2013.
10 MacDonald, 2013.
11 Holden Caulfield is the protagonist anti-hero in J.D. Salinger's 1951 novel, *Catcher in the Rye* (2010). Chapman was still holding a copy when New York police arrested him.
12 McMahon, 2020.
13 Boyd, 2016. In 1998, Bowie, a then board member of *Modern Painters* and co-director of 21 Publishing, published a biography titled: *Nat Tate: An American Artist 1928–1960*. While presented as the discovery of a talented abstract expressionist, Nat Tate was entirely fictional, a character born of the imagination of its mischievous author, William Boyd (Boyd, 2020).
14 Middleton, 1985, p. 203.
15 Kivy, 1995, p. 1.
16 Critchley, 2014, p. 41.
17 Buckley, 2005, p. 139.
18 Von Appen and Doehring, 2006, p. 38, n 16.
19 Savage, 2005.
20 Johnson, 2015, p. 12.
21 Crowe, 1976b.
22 Brown, 2017. While Bowie might be, and often has been, described as postmodern, we should recognise his artistic straddling of the modern/postmodern divide. After all, postmodernism can be viewed as a 'pose' and Bowie as "posing as postmodern" (Baker, 2015, p. 106). Moreover, Bowie's art never became "pure 'signature' in the Warholian sense" (Baker, 2015, p. 108). That is, the modernist idea of the singer-songwriter as genius remained important to fan and critical appreciation of Bowie, even if his genius was increasingly inflected through a Burroughsian lens (see the fourth essay in this collection which considers the influence of William Burroughs on Bowie's creative output).
23 Trilling, 1972.
24 Hegel, 2002, p. 515.
25 Jean Jacques Rousseau pioneered the development of philosophical romanticism (Rousseau, 1973) and Charles Lindholm has described him as the inventor of modern authenticity (Lindholm, 2008). 'Authenticity,' as a philosophical idea, was subsequently developed by a number of important figures, including Nietzsche (1974), Heidegger (1978) and Sartre (2018).
26 Key literary figures within the English Romantic movement (1790–1850) include William Wordsworth, Percy Bysshe Shelley, John Keats and Mary Shelley (2010).
27 Keightley, 2001; Lindberg et al, 2005.
28 Taylor, 1989.
29 Taylor, 1991. In Taylor's view, this shift away from public to private selves represents a problem because it has involved a retreat from community and, especially since the 1960s, has led to narcissistic self-indulgence (p. 12). See also Christopher Lasch (1979) and Allan Bloom (1987).
30 Rubridge, 1996, p. 219.
31 Kivy, 1995.
32 Weisethaunet and Lindberg, 2010, pp. 472–473.
33 Shuker, 2012, p. 23.
34 Potter, 2020; Pratt, 1986.
35 Weinstein, 1999.
36 Mazillo, 2000, p. 715.
37 Phillips, 1997, pp. 5–6.

38 Fox, 2016, p. 59.
39 Foucault, 1972, p. 17.
40 Foucault, 1980b, p. 60.
41 Foucault, 1988b, p. 49.
42 Crowe, 1976a.
43 Usher and Fremaux, 2015, p. 75.
44 Critchley, 2014, p. 26.
45 Taylor, 1989.
46 'Andy Warhol' (*Hunky Dory* album, 1971 RCA).
47 Brackett, 2005, p. 279.
48 McLuhan, 1964.
49 Critchley, 2014, p. 54.
50 Reisch, 2016, p. 6.
51 Rossinow, 1998, p. 345.
52 Woody Guthrie was an American singer-songwriter considered to be one of the most significant figures in American folk music (see Cray, 2006).
53 Baker, 2015, p. 105.
54 As Bowie explained in his 1974 interview with William Burroughs, he wanted to create an immediacy of experience (Copetas, 1973).
55 Trynka, 2011, p. 151.
56 The term refers to an artistic practice for transforming artworks through disfiguring them in creative ways.
57 Debord, 1994, p. 11.
58 Weisethaunet and Lindberg, 2010.
59 Grossberg, 1993, p. 206.
60 Moore, 2002, p. 210.
61 Fornäs, 1995, pp. 116–117.
62 'All the Young Dudes' (written by Bowie for Mott the Hoople, *All the Young Dudes* album, 1972 CBS/Columbia).
63 *Space Oddity* album 1969 (Philips/Mercury).
64 'God' (*John Lennon/Plastic Ono Band* album, 1970 Apple).
65 Rorabaugh, 2015.
66 Taylor, 1991; Lasch, 1979.
67 Peraino, 2012, p. 155.
68 'Janine' (*Space Oddity* album, 1969 Philips/Mercury).
69 'Wild Eyed Boy from Freecloud' (*Space Oddity* album, 1969 Philips/Mercury).
70 Critchley, 2014, p. 116.
71 Bowie described originality as one of the most overrated virtues (Vanity Fair, 2016).
72 Curcio, 2020, p. 13.
73 Barthes, 1967.
74 Brooker, 2019, p. 89. Indeed, Bowie himself observed "[t]here's no new way of saying anything" (Crowe, 1976a).
75 Bowie, 1995.
76 Roberts, 1995.
77 Bowie has claimed that he often preferred fans' interpretations of his lyrics (Copetas, 1974).
78 Marcel Duchamp was a French-American painter, sculptor and writer whose work is associated with Cubism, Dada and conceptual art (see Bass, 2019).
79 Paxman, 1999. See also Littman, 2016.
80 Barthes, 1967, p. 148.
81 Brooker, 2019, p. 89.
82 See Richard Fitch for a rich discussion of this theme in Bowie's lyrics (2015).
83 Critchley, 2014, p. 26.
84 Bowie is a name he assumed in 1969. Bowie's legal name was David Jones. The change of name was to avoid confusion with Davy Jones, the English lead singer of the US band, the *Monkees*.

85 *The Rise and Fall of Ziggy Stardust and the Spiders from Mars* album, 1972 RCA.
86 *Aladdin Sane* album, 1973 RCA. While there is overlap between the Ziggy and Aladdin Sane characters, Bowie explained "Ziggy was meant to be clearly cut out and well defined with areas of interplay whereas Aladdin is pretty ephemeral" (Shaar Murray, 1973).
87 *Diamond Dogs* album, 1974 RCA.
88 *Young Americans* album, 1975 RCA.
89 Bowie's Thin White Duke phase traversed albums but was most associated with the 1976 album, *Station to Station* RCA.
90 Nietzsche, 1974.
91 *Scary Monsters* album, 1980 RCA.
92 Saint Clair, 2002, p. 216.
93 The Droogs were a violent anti-social gang in Kubrick's 1971 film. The film was based on Anthony Burgess' 1962 novel of the same name.
94 The Legendary Stardust Cowboy was the stage name of Norman Carl Odam. He was an outsider performer and pioneer of the genre that became known as psychobilly, a fusion of rockabilly and punk rock (Buckley, 2005, pp. 110–111).
95 See the following essay where this theme will be developed in the context of the relationship between art, aesthetics and ethics.
96 Lindsay Kemp was a mime and leader of the Lindsay Kemp troupe. Bowie was one of his students, and for a time lover, in the late 1960s.
97 Auslander, 2006, p. 106.
98 Jones, 2012, p. 171.
99 Quoted by Usher and Fremaux, 2015, p. 58.
100 White, 1978.
101 Lampert, 2016, p. 152.
102 Critchley, 2014, p. 115.
103 Critchley, 2014, p. 54.
104 *Diamond Dogs* album, 1974 RCA. These songs will be considered in more depth in the fourth essay in this collection.
105 Gill, 2016.
106 Holm-Hudson, 2018, p. 214.
107 We will consider Bowie's use of cut-up lyrics in depth in the fourth essay in this collection.
108 Critchley, 2016, p. 170. This book is an updated version of Critchley's 2014 *Bowie*, written after Bowie's death and the release of his final album, *Blackstar* ISO/Columbia/Sony.

Ethics

3

'FLIRTING' WITH FASCISM

The Thin White Duke, art and ethical limits

Introduction

This essay considers the relationship between transgressive art and ethics and, in particular, ethical objections to transgressive art. Objections can take several forms. These include perceived offence to bourgeoise sensibilities (the photography of Robert Mapplethorpe),[1] a view of art as harmful, for example, because it is considered to condone child abuse (Nabokov's *Lolita*)[2] or art may be considered blasphemous (Serrano's *Piss Christ*)[3] or anti-semitic (Wagner's *Ring*).[4] However, in considering art's relationship to ethics, this essay is not concerned with questions of offence, harm or censorship.[5] In lieu of such normative, empirical and/or politico-philosophical questions, it considers what has been described as "an *intrinsic* relation between art and morality,"[6] or to be more specific, the relationship between "the aesthetic and the ethical values of artworks."[7] This focus serves to prioritise the following questions: (1) is the aesthetic value of an artwork conditioned by its ethical properties? (2) If so, is this true in all or only some contexts? and (3) Where true, does this mean ethically defective artworks are necessarily aesthetically diminished?

These questions will be explored through the vehicle of David Bowie, and more particularly, through one of his 1970s reincarnations, the Thin White Duke. This Bowie character comes to the fore in the present context for two reasons: first, because during his Thin White Duke period, Bowie was accused of flirting with fascism;[8] second, because the music he produced, its artistic presentation and the sublime affect it had on his audience, make this period of Bowie's creative output stand out as exceptional. In other words, some of Bowie's greatest work drew on National Socialism, or at least, its theatricality and other artistic props. That is, Bowie adopted a fascist icon character and built his 1976 Isolar world tour, at least in part, around national socialist stagecraft,[9] the implications of which the essay will explore. To be clear, the Bowie 'artwork' to be considered is not a single object,

DOI: 10.4324/9781003140429-7

like a Dickens novel or a Picasso painting. Rather, it contains several elements. These include visual and musical performance, set design and lighting, Bowie's Thin White Duke character, and his *Station to Station* album[10] which drove the tour ('the artwork').[11] In considering Bowie's artwork in ethical terms, these elements must be considered in their totality. However, before doing so, and in order to do so, I will first provide an ethical framework for evaluating artworks.

An ethical framework for evaluating artworks

There is a long-standing debate within the philosophy of art and art criticism concerning the proper relationship between art and ethics. This is due largely to the fact that the powers of art "have made it the recurrent object of high ethical hope and of deep ethical concern."[12] After all, art goes to the heart of who we are. It plays a significant role in the development of our emotional lives, how we think about ourselves, and the world in which we live. As part of this debate, various philosophical arguments have been offered in order to answer the kind of questions posed. The three main contemporary philosophical positions are, as Berys Gaut notes: *moralism*, *autonomism* and *immoralism*.[13] These various positions involve complex sets of arguments concerned with the question of whether "there are more or less appropriate ways of appreciating individual artworks."[14] Given the essay form adopted here, I can only offer an overview of some of their main properties.

Moralism tends to be animated by pedagogic concerns pertaining to whether artworks are considered morally uplifting or corrosive,[15] and it contends moral defects hinder full cognitive and/or emotional engagement with, or psychological uptake of, an artwork.[16] It does not claim ethics to be the only or most important means of evaluating an artwork's aesthetic value. On the contrary, it recognises form, content, harmony and other aesthetic values must also be considered. Moreover, moralism acknowledges ethically meritorious art can be, and often is, banal (in the case of literature, pedestrian prose, weak characterisation, unnecessary sentimentality and so forth). Nevertheless, it espouses the view ethical merits of works of art contribute to their aesthetic value, while ethical defects count against. Given our focus on ethical defects, let me restate moralism's claim: an artwork is to some degree aesthetically diminished if ethically defective. However, this is only the case *sometimes* for at least two reasons. First, in order that the importance of ethics to the assessment of art not be trivialised, it must be made subject to a *de minimis* principle. That is, ethical defects ought only to count against an artwork where they are significant. Second, ethical defects or merits of artworks only count where they are considered 'aesthetically relevant.' Of course, this begs the question: when are ethical properties 'aesthetically relevant?' I will come to this issue shortly but first let me introduce the other broad philosophical positions.

Autonomism strives to uncouple art from ethics. While an artwork may in some sense be ethically defective, autonomism views this as irrelevant in assessing its aesthetic worth. It is really another term for aestheticism or, in common parlance, an endorsement of the adage, 'art for art's sake.'[17] Autonomism, which is often expressed in formalistic terms, as a concern with form rather than the substance of artworks, has few modern adherents. While it was championed in the 1950s by the New Critics,[18] who shared T. S. Eliot's view that it is self-evident "a creation, a work of art, is autonomous,"[19] it has been subjected to sustained feminist,[20] critical race[21] and postcolonial critique.[22] While a case might be made for it in relation to artworks like side two of Bowie's 1977 *Low* album, which is not only instrumental but devoid of passion, cool and intellectual, few artworks are easily separated from their substance, their context, their passions. This is certainly true of Bowie's 1976 Isolar world tour and his *Station to Station* album.

Finally, immoralism captures the idea of art as transgression or estrangement. As Daniel Jacobson notes, it adopts the view ethical defects *can* contribute to an artwork's aesthetic worth, while ethical merits *can* diminish it.[23] This view may seem counter-intuitive. In order to grasp it, it is necessary to recognise immoralism defends ethical defects in artworks on the basis of their capacity to deepen our moral understanding. It might be considered a form of moralism by stealth as the claim ethical defects enhance artworks in aesthetic terms tends to be at its strongest, its most coherent, its most persuasive, where ethical defects serve a moral purpose. As Émile Durkheim recognised long ago, transgression not only challenges the moral law, it brings it into view.[24] One of its functions is to remind us of moral boundaries, and in the process, in the moment of transgressing them, prop them up. Or as Anthony Julius has put it: "artworks, which are ethically problematic, in time return the reader or viewer, somewhat clearer-eyed, to the regularities of the briefly transgressed code."[25] Moreover, while transgression can serve to bolster the law which requires it,[26] it can also and simultaneously shine a light on what is wrong with society, that is, tease out, and thereby challenge, immorality. In this sense, immoralism can be understood not in terms of condoning evil but as an artistic approach that plays a role in helping to constitute moral selves. Indeed, art that calls into question conventional wisdom, the self-evident, the axiomatic, might be viewed as playing a vital role in improving the moral well-being of society.

Unlike artworks that convey a relatively clear moral lesson, artworks that might be defended from an immoralist perspective tend to be more opaque when it comes to determining any moral content they may possess. This is because such artworks aim at defamiliarisation, rendering us "exiles from the known."[27] They unsettle us, shake us out of our complacency, enlarge our sense of what is possible. At their most sublime, and as noted by Kant, they defeat our understanding but in doing so expose us to its limits, thereby enlarging our understanding.[28] While their opacity might be considered to count against such artworks ethically speaking, immoralists argue that in denying us "the pleasures of easy recognition"[29] they require us to work harder, to participate more fully in an artwork, and that this serves to enlarge our critical faculties and moral sensibilities.

As Matthew Kieran notes, moral knowledge cannot be reduced to a set of prescriptions or propositions. Rather, it requires the development of a skill or capacity. And this type of skill, Kieran views as capable of deepening our moral understanding and appreciation, can be developed through "imaginatively experiencing morally defective cognitive-affective responses and attitudes in ways that are morally problematic."[30] In other words, our moral understanding can be enriched through immersing ourselves in a morally problematic artwork and suspending, at least temporarily, our moral judgment. In short, immoralism, and perhaps the estrangement defence, in particular, "depends upon, without [always] acknowledging, a residual pedagogic/moral case for art."[31]

However, some philosophers have articulated what has been described as a more "robust immoralism,"[32] one that defends ethical defects irrespective of any moral payoff. According to this position, ethical defects are considered to improve the aesthetic value of artworks irrespective of any role they play in constituting moral selves. As Anne Eaton explains in the context of the novel's antihero, ethical defects "can overcome the audience's imaginative resistance"[33] and this overcoming "takes considerable artistry and finesse" because "[t]he character must be convincingly monstrous or depraved yet simultaneously likeable, sympathetic, and even admirable."[34] However, the notion this approach dispenses with morality appears dubious. Thus, in developing her argument, Eaton explains that an immoral artwork develops imaginative resistance but in a way which "keeps that resistance in play so that we continually feel its pull. In this way, [an artwork] trades on our moral convictions while simultaneously turning us against them, thereby putting us in conflict with ourselves."[35]

Dividing us against ourselves is considered aesthetically valuable because it draws us into a "protracted state of ambivalence,"[36] something which makes an artwork compelling. As Eaton puts it: "we are captivated by and savour this ambivalence; it makes these works haunt us and keep us awake at night."[37] Yet, a focus on ambivalence draws us back to morality. After all, ambivalence is not indifference or complicity. It encourages reflection and might be viewed as an ethical posture that resists drift toward moral and political certainties. It is an attitude borne of recognition of complexity, of something too big to frame. It invites curiosity, humility and openness. As Hili Razinsky notes, "[i]n questions of value, ambivalence can be the best way to appreciate a situation" because "opposed attitudes can be better (richer, more sincere, more appropriate, more sensitive) for their opposition."[38]

Having provided an overview of some of the main properties of moralism, autonomism and immoralism, I now return to an issue identified earlier, namely, the issue of 'aesthetic relevance.' You will recall that ethical properties, even where significant, *only* diminish or enhance artworks, aesthetically speaking, where they are aesthetically relevant. Defining 'aesthetic relevance,' however, is not a matter of consensus. For the purpose of this essay, I will adopt Gaut's view of aesthetic relevance. On his account, ethical defects or merits of artworks are aesthetically relevant where "ethical attitudes [are] manifested in the responses (these being affective-cognitive states) *that works prescribe their audiences to have*."[39] Putting it more succinctly, Gaut asks us to consider whether an artwork "get[s] us to *feel* the force of a particular claim or truth," that is, does it "bring it home to us."[40] Discussing Gaut's position, Andrea Sauchelli puts it this way: "if the moral character of a work of art is relevant to the *appreciation* of the work of art itself," it is aesthetically relevant.[41] In other words, where an artwork requires, encourages or invites a particular cognitive and/or emotional response "toward persons, actions, events [or] situations,"[42] then it has an ethical attitude relevant to its aesthetic evaluation.

To summarise the argument so far, artworks often have ethical properties. These properties can be ethical defects or ethical merits. However, such properties only become important to the aesthetic evaluation of artworks where they are considered aesthetically relevant.[43] To be aesthetically relevant, ethical properties must have an attitude which audiences are invited to adopt. If they do, it must be determined whether it is a moral or immoral attitude. At this point, things become more complicated because defining an attitude as immoral is far from straightforward as our consideration of immoralism has revealed. Indeed, in most, if not all cases, artworks defended by immoralists tend to bear a positive if somewhat circuitous relationship to morality. If the morality of such artworks differs from those more readily accounted for by moralism, this is perhaps an effect of the different methods they adopt to communicate moral ideas or concerns to their audiences and/or a matter of degree. I will argue Bowie's artwork can be defended from an immoralist perspective, that is, its ethical defects can be considered to contribute to its aesthetic value. Before developing this claim, however, I will first provide some detail concerning Bowie's artwork.

The Thin White Duke and fascism

David Bowie was fascinated by the Nazis, their mythology, their imagery,[44] their "dramatisation of power,"[45] or to quote Walter Benjamin, their "aestheticization of politics."[46] His fascination appears to have been informed by his interest in hermetic Qabalah[47] and the fact aspects of Nazi ideology had their roots in the occult,[48] and by the fact he was always drawn first to the image, not the word. Bowie considered the Nazis to have had "the most powerful set of symbols that have ever been invoked in terms of political history."[49] His interest in the Nazis and the totalitarian mindset was not new. It is evident in his earlier work. It first finds expression on the song 'Quicksand,'[50] which appears to have Adolf Hitler as narrator, stuck in the bunker ('the ragged hole') considering suicide ('should I kiss the viper's fang'). While he does so, he reflects bitterly on betrayals ('I'm the twisted name on Garbo's eyes,[51] living proof of Churchill's lies') and tries to come to terms with the fact power has ultimately eluded him ('I ain't got the power anymore').[52] However, Bowie's exploration of totalitarianism is most notable on *Diamond Dogs*, which is essentially a musical version of George Orwell's *1984*, though Bowie had experienced messiah worship with Ziggy, particularly on the US tour, and had admitted to getting lost in it.[53]

With his latest incarnation, the Thin White Duke, a persona Bowie assumed in late 1975, he wanted to explore further the relationship between audience and star, charismatic leader and followers. As the Duke, his exploration of this theme homed in not on imagined dystopian futures as in the past but on the conjuring up of a very specific and traumatic past for present artistic purposes. The Duke has been described variously as "a mad aristocrat,"[54] "an amoral zombie,"[55] and "an emotionless Aryan superman,"[56] and by Bowie himself, as "[a] very Aryan fascist type."[57] Such assessments were informed and/or consolidated by the fact the Duke had "sculpted cheeks, dyed [blond/red] hair swept back across his head, stern black costume – that encapsulated Hitler's vision of the perfect Aryan icon,"[58] and by the fact his dapper aristocratic look bore resemblance to well-known Nazi sympathiser, and fellow (post-abdication) Duke, Edward VIII.[59]

A view of the Duke as fascist, or as a figure sympathetic to fascism, finds further support in a number of media interviews the Duke gave during 1976.[60] The reader may think a focus on the Duke, rather than on Bowie, is disingenuous and serves as an attempt to exculpate Bowie from appropriate criticism and moral censure. However, we need to recognise the Duke is part of the artwork and that Bowie immersed himself in the Duke in the fashion of a method actor, as he had done with earlier characters like Ziggy. And while Bowie's intentions certainly assist us in understanding the attitude of his artwork, shed light on the direction and purpose of his latest artistic turn, it is the attitude of his artwork, not his intent, that is to be judged. Let us turn to some of the statements made by the Duke, one's which provide a window onto Bowie's artistic project.

In an interview in *Playboy Magazine*, it was suggested to him that he believed very strongly in fascism. The Duke agreed, adding:

> [t]he only way we can speed up the sort of liberalism that's hanging foul in the air at the moment is to speed up the progress of a right-wing, totally dictatorial tyranny and get it over as fast as possible.[61]

Turning away from his call for the arrival of dictatorship, the installing of Big Brother, the Duke provided further insight. Thus, he stated, "Adolf Hitler was one of the first rock stars."[62] When asked to clarify what he meant by this startling remark, he added:

> [l]ook at some of his films and see how he moved. I think he was quite as good as Jagger. It's astounding. And, boy, when he hit that stage, he worked an audience. Good God! He was no politician. He was a media artist himself. He used politics and theatrics and created this thing that governed and controlled the show for those 12 years. The world will never see his like again. He staged a country.[63]

Tactless and insensitive as these comments may be considered to be, they are hardly random. Rather, they foreground the power dynamic Bowie wanted to explore, one between audience and star. Moreover, Bowie was always in touch with the present moment, one that had witnessed "a resurgence of interest in fascism and Nazism. The compromises and shames of the war, the allure of fascist imagery."[64] Remember Bertolucci's *The Conformist* 1970, Cavani's *The Night Porter* 1974, Pasolini's *Salo* 1975.[65] And in Britain, the National Front were gaining ground and swastika-wearing punks were just around the corner.[66] While on occasion, Bowie sought to distance himself from the Duke's comments[67] and to attribute them to the effects of cocaine,[68] this appears to have been due to his desire to put lingering accusations of fascism behind him rather than a genuine disavowal of their relevance to his artistic project.[69] Equally, while Bowie and/as the Duke could be playful,[70] this should not detract from his serious intent. As Bowie stated in 1977, "my job is as an observer of what is happening and any statements I made [about fascism] were a general reaction and a theatrical observation of what I could see happening in England."[71] Moreover, as already noted, Bowie's interest in fascism and totalitarianism more generally were long-standing and certainly preceded his legendary cocaine habit.

Importantly, Bowie understood the power stars wield, especially rock stars. Having achieved fame, he began, as Kevin Hill has noted, "to see parallels between the celebrity he sought within a liberal society, and the role of the political leader . . . and at the limit, the totalitarian leader."[72] As he explained in 1974, "[t]here are times, frankly, when I could have told the audience to do anything, and that's frightening."[73] Shifting attention to the theme of decadence, the Duke insisted "morals should be straightened up for a start. They're disgusting."[74] Later, in a more revealing moment, where he suspends his method acting in order to reflect on his and other rock stars' gender performances, Bowie stated "with our makeup and funny clothes . . . I feel that we're only heralding something darker than ourselves."[75] In other words, while talking about rock 'n' roll excess, he alluded to a cultural milieu that prefigured German fascism.[76]

Like Michel Foucault, Bowie seemed to grasp the fact fascism is in all of us, "in our heads and in our everyday behavior. . . [that it] . . . causes us to love power, to desire the very thing that dominates and exploits us,"[77] and that it is, at least in part, "anchored in the body, in desire and the emotions."[78] Just a year earlier, Bowie exhibited "anxious reflection"[79] on such questions of power on his *Young Americans* album. As he noted, 'fame, makes a man take things over,' and in placing distance between himself and its trappings, 'fame, puts you there where things are hollow.'[80] He also understood how the desire for some brave Apollo tends to trump the desire for individual freedom, how dependency and submission assume appeal in the face of its heavy burden.[81] Echoing Eric Fromm's view of the attraction of totalitarianism as "flight from freedom,"[82] as "longing for submission,"[83] the Duke stated:

> [people] say they want freedom, but when they get the chance, they pass up Nietzsche and choose Hitler, because he would march into a room to speak and music and lights would come on at strategic moments. It was rather like a rock 'n' roll concert. The kids would get very excited – girls got hot and sweaty and guys wished it was them up there. That, for me, is the rock 'n' roll experience.[84]

In other words, rock 'n' roll or at least some (the best) examples of it are likened to a Nuremberg rally. Bowie wanted to stage an encounter between rock star and audience that would capture something of this highly charged mood, one of excitement and danger, in order to explore the relationship between rock star as charismatic leader and audience as followers, as those who give themselves over to power.

In terms of his performance, Bowie disoriented his audience first by showing the 1929 surrealist short film by Luis Buñuel and Salvador Dalí, *Un Chien Andalou*, which includes a famous scene of a razor blade cutting into a woman's eyeball.[85] Bowie's use of *Un Chien Andalou* is revealing because the film privileges the image over everything else and in this sense gestures toward a fascism incipient at the time of its making. Buñuel and Dalí had insisted "[n]o idea or image that might lend itself to a rational explanation of any kind" would make the cut.[86] In other words, through a nightmarish dream-logic, the audience were introduced to a world beyond reason, to a world of repressed desires. We should also recognise that while the film was designed to scandalise its audience, it failed to do so,[87] causing Buñuel to express frustration with "the inane herd that saw beauty or poetry in something which was basically no more than a desperate impassioned call for murder."[88]

While the audience processed the film, which had been accompanied by futuristic music care of Kraftwerk's *Radioactivity*, absent the quartet, the Duke appeared on a stage devoid of props and other visual distractions.[89] The spectacle was stark: the Duke and Gitanes cigarettes;[90] black and white expressionism; waistcoat and slicked back blonde/red hair. And all framed by enormous banks of fluorescent, "almost painful to the eyes,"[91] white light. As Bowie biographer, David Buckley notes, "[m]any journalists witnessing the 1976 Bowie tour remembered old footage of the Nuremberg rallies and the dramatically creative use of white light to illuminate *der Fuhrer*."[92] While Bowie was clearly influenced by the art and sensibility of Weimar Republican decadence,[93] which the Nazis hated, his stagecraft cannot be reduced to Brechtian theatre or *Cabaret*. Leni Riefenstahl is here too. Like the armies depicted in her Nazi propaganda film, *Triumph of the Will*,[94] Bowie's theatricality emphasised strength and power. Having built "a crescendo of dramatic intensity"[95] much like Riefenstahl's film, and "[a] mood of both futurism and nostalgia [having] flooded the arena,"[96] the Duke opened the set list with the song, 'Station to Station,' a ten-minute monster that builds for over three minutes before his vocal kicks in.

While the song's title alludes to the fourteen stations of the Christian Cross,[97] to Jesus' journey from Gethsemane to Calvary, it and the song's lyrics were more informed by hermetic Qabalah and the Tree of Life.[98] Musically, however, the metaphor was experienced as a locomotive train inching one's way. As Peter Doggett notes, "the train was no express, bound for glory; its lumbering progress suggested a force too evil to stop,"[99] something wicked this way comes. And, of course, given what we know about the Duke, it is difficult to think of the train without imagining the final solution. The slow instrumental build produced a hypnotic effect on the audience with lead guitarist, Earl Slick, using feedback to sustain a single note for what seemed like an eternity.[100] Finally, the Duke began to sing:

'The return of the Thin White Duke, throwing darts in lovers eyes, here are we, one magical moment, such is the stuff, from where dreams are woven.'[101] Lyrically the song is opaque, an effect of Bowie's use of William Burroughs' cut-ups writing technique.[102] However, while the song suggests more than it reveals, it evokes the Nazi mindset, particularly the quasi-religious Nazi paganism that looked back to ancient roots and forward to manifest destiny. As the tour progressed, audiences were "on the verge of hysteria"[103] and Bowie's greatest music critic, Lester Bangs,[104] described the *Station to Station* album, which the tour had promoted, as Bowie's "first masterpiece."[105]

Judging Bowie's artwork

In order to judge an artwork's ethical attitude, that is, to pinpoint what it encourages or invites, we must consider the artwork itself, any relevant contexts, including its historical context, and (where information is available) the artist's intent.[106] It is for this reason that judgment about ethical properties of artworks must be made from an informed perspective. A focus on an artwork's ethical attitude as opposed to an artist's intent reflects this essay's focus on an intrinsic relation between aesthetic and ethical values.[107] While motive or intent may assume relevance, may shed light on the attitude expressed in an artwork, it is the attitude expressed, one which an artwork invites an audience to take up, irrespective of whether it succeeds in doing so, that matters. Adopting Gaut's definition, it is conceded Bowie's artwork has 'aesthetically relevant' ethical properties. That is, it is accepted the moral character of Bowie's artwork is relevant to its appreciation. This is because it deals with fascism and more general questions of totalitarianism and, in particular, the relationship between the leader and her followers, between power and desire, and because, through stagecraft, musical and lyrical composition, and the character of the Duke, it registers these things emotionally.

Importantly, ethical questions arise concerning the attitude expressed in Bowie's artwork toward these things, not least because of what might be seen as ambiguity toward a traumatic historical scene. It is immoralism that best captures and provides a defence for Bowie's artwork. Judged from the perspective of immoralism, which seeks to elevate at least some forms of transgressive art in aesthetic terms, ethical defects in Bowie's artwork can be viewed as enhancing rather than diminishing the aesthetic value of his artwork. This might be because his artwork can be considered to advance morality by stealth in the sense of a somewhat opaque but morally positive (anti-fascist) message or because its attitude bears a certain ambivalence about its subject matter (desire for power and its refusal), bearing in mind the positive moral value ambivalence can have. In my view, both readings are open to us.

While Bowie's artwork invites audiences to engage with a traumatic historical scene, its attitude does not affirm fascism. In terms of its lyrics, the song 'Station to Station' does not celebrate power, racial or otherwise. While it entreats the audience to 'Drink to the men who protect you and I, Drink, drink, drain your glass, raise your glass high,' which might be thought to have fascist overtones, the song ultimately calls for love ('I'm thinking that it must be love'), not hate, but either way '[i]t's too late' for the 'European canon is here.' The phrase 'European canon' is a rich one and appears to refer to several things: a shift in Bowie's gaze away from America and perhaps a reaffirmation of his European identity; recognition of the Germanic lands as the cradle of eighteenth- and nineteenth-century classical music, (Bach, Mozart, Beethoven, Wagner, Offenbach, Bruckner, Mahler) as well as music of more recent origin (Weill, Orff, Stockhausen, Kraftwerk, Neu); and, perhaps crucially, a recognition of Europe's political legacy as one of trauma, the scene of the spilling of much blood.

The song, 'Station to Station,' characterised the mood and power of the tour. Through it, and the artwork more generally, Bowie does not suture European wounds. He lays them bare. He provides a portal onto an historical scene. Audiences sensed the energy, emotions ran high, there was a sense of Nuremberg but no endorsement of fascism. In the opening lines of 'Station to Station,' we learn the Duke has returned, perhaps from exile like Hitler in the 1920s. As you will recall, his first action is to '[throw] darts in lovers' eyes.' Darts are a reference to the conflict between God and the devil, and specifically to the devil's choice of weaponry. As Saint Paul explains in his Letter to the Ephesians, with "the shield of faith . . . you will be able to quench all the fiery darts of the wicked one."[108] However, the battle to which the song alludes is ultimately a human affair, an internal struggle between love of power and its refusal. The artwork, however, does not nurture this love.

While the Duke croons 'wish upon, wish upon, day upon day, I believe oh Lord, I believe all the way'[109] and, in an obvious reference to Hitler's Reich, 'I'll stick with you baby for a thousand years,'[110] in the face of this impending nightmare, he urges us to 'run for the shadows,'[111] not embrace what is on offer. And, of course, Bowie's artwork, unlike Nazi propaganda, offers no clear message, no sense of unity, any fascist bonds created lasting just for one day. The Duke is no saviour, no Siegfried.[112] Rather, he appears to be a somewhat lost soul ('Got to keep searching and searching, And oh, what will I be believing').[113] While Riefenstahl had a clear ideological vision, which was the very essence of her film,[114] Bowie's artwork offers only lyrical opacity against the backdrop of confounding sounds and visions. It offers no prescriptions or solutions, other than perhaps to think for ourselves.

Through the artwork, Bowie aimed to engage psychologically in an exploration of power relations between leader (star) and followers (audience), a dynamic he had identified as lying at the heart of the rock 'n' roll experience, and with which fans would have been familiar given his earlier explorations of this theme through his *Ziggy Stardust* and *Diamond Dogs* albums and tours. With the 1976 Isolar tour, Bowie aimed artistically to intensify this dynamic. In exploring this "dark night of the soul,"[115] he did not attempt to replicate Nuremberg, but he did capture something of that time and place for artistic effect. While Bowie's artwork is not an exorcism or banishment of a fascist mindset,[116] nor designed to produce this effect, I do not share James Curcio's view that exorcism is the *only* place where transgression finds its justification.[117] It is also important, at least sometimes, to simply stare into the abyss, and encourage audiences to do the same, though, as Nietzsche recognised, it might stare right back at you.[118] Bowie's artwork does not attempt to sell us fascist ideology, but it does rely on Nazi stagecraft and music with slow menace in order to create a sense of awe. The artwork unsettles, estranges us from the familiar, yet at the same time returns us to it. That is, it holds up a mirror to the fascist in each and every fan and in each and every one of us. In this respect, Bowie's artwork assumes a morality that elevates it in aesthetic terms.

However, the aesthetically relevant ethical properties in Bowie's artwork are not confined to an invitation to "imaginatively experienc[e] morally defective cognitive-affective responses and attitudes."[119] Rather, they also include the undermining of fascism through the mixing of genre. Thus, in contrast to the Nazi vision of racial purity, Bowie's artwork offers hybridity, here in the form of an album and tour that fused European electronic music (which he would later develop with Brian Eno)[120] and black American funk (in which he had immersed himself on his *Young Americans* album). While he sang of 'Golden Years,' he did so to a disco beat, thereby undercutting fascist ideology. As Doggett notes, through the song, Bowie offered an "intensely hypnotic weave of electronic certainty and human vulnerability."[121] Indeed, in retrospect, Bowie emerges as central to the cross-fertilisation of these different musical forms and to their subsequent hybridical proliferation. As rock journalist, Paul Du Noyer, has pointed out, Bowie foreshadowed an "impending [musical] sea change,"[122] a beautiful mongrelisation that would set the tone for the next twenty years.

Conclusion

In my view, Bowie's artwork is not unethical, in a significant sense, when considered in its entirety and from the perspective of immoralism. The ethical defects in his artwork serve to strengthen it in the sense of its capacity to produce estrangement and reflection and perhaps bring us to our (heightened) senses. Ultimately, Bowie's artwork does not "tempt us to find attractive what is morally repugnant."[123] It does not solicit our complicity. Rather, it disorientates us in order to challenge our notions of rock and art, politics and culture and, of course, ourselves, our desire for power.

Of course, if an artwork is ethically defective when considered as a whole, this ought to occasion reflection on the part of those who remain moved by it. For ethical criteria ought to apply to the realm of feeling as well as action because art can move us affectively.[124] However, the feelings Bowie's artwork produces are not ethically defective in a significant sense because heightened feeling is a merited response. That is, not only did the 1976 Isolar world tour and the *Station to Station* album provide experiences of the sublime in terms of their more general aesthetic properties. These experiences are also merited in the ethical sense for the reasons discussed. After all, while his claim to have caricatured fascism[125] perhaps rings hollow in view of his seductive performances,[126] it is fair to say his artwork addressed a contemporary, and age-old problem, concerning the human condition. As Bowie himself puts it in response to accusations of fascism:[127]

> I'm Pierrot. I'm Everyman. What I'm doing is theatre, and only theatre. . . . What you see on stage isn't sinister. It's pure clown. I'm using myself as a canvas and trying to paint the truth of our time on it. The white face, the baggy pants – they're Pierrot, the eternal clown putting over the great sadness of 1976.[128]

And a year later, as questions about his attitude to fascism persisted: "the best leader [people] can possibly have is the one that looks back at them from the mirror."[129]

Notes

1 *The Perfect Moment* exhibition 1989, a retrospective of Mapplethorpe's work featuring sado-masochistic gay male imagery, led to an escalation of the confrontation between the US Congress and the National Endowment for the Arts, which led to Congress prohibiting federal funding of 'obscene' or 'homoerotic art' (Sturzaker and Sturzaker, 1975; Stychin, 1995, Chp 1).

2 Vladimir Nabokov's novel has proved especially controversial. It was banned in the UK and France at the time of its release in 1955 (Nabokov, 2000). While many critics consider it a literary masterpiece, it continues to provoke controversy given it deals with the ongoing sexual abuse of a twelve-year old girl, Dolores Haze ('Lolita').

3 The 1989 artwork, *Piss Christ*, by Andres Serrano, presents an image of Christ in urine. This provocative artwork also played a role in the decision of the US Congress to restrict federal funding of the National Endowment for the Arts (Stychin, 1995, Chp 1).

4 The composer, Richard Wagner, was a well-known anti-semite and his *Ring* and other works have proved controversial because of what many critics see as an attitude of anti-semitism inherent within such works (Geck, 2013; Adorno, 2005; Gutman, 1990). His operas have never been performed in the State of Israel.

5 However, a desire to censor often comes to the fore once an artwork is judged to be morally defective in some way.

6 Gaut, 2007, p. 8.

7 Gaut, 2007, p. 34.

8 Musician's Union, 1976; Jones, 1977.

9 The tour, which commenced on 2 February 1976 and launched the *Station to Station* album which was released on 23 January 1976, was also referred to as the Thin White Duke tour and the White Light tour. It is not to be confused with Bowie's second Isolar tour in 1978.

10 1976 RCA.

11 Debates concerning the proper relationship between art and ethics have tended to focus on works of literature. This has been due to what is considered a more obvious connection between the written word and moral education. Nevertheless, and while some artworks, especially some forms of instrumental music, may lie beyond meaningful ethical criticism, a wide variety of artworks can be considered to possess aesthetically relevant ethical properties.

12 Gaut, 2007, p. 1.

13 Gaut, 2007, pp. 10–11. There are radical and moderate versions of these various positions as Gaut notes. Gaut himself has developed a philosophical position which he describes as *ethicism*. Ethicism, at least in theory, is a stricter version of moralism. We will not deal with ethicism in this essay.

14 Schellekens, 2020.
15 Notable exponents of this view include Leo Tolstoy (1930), John Ruskin (Atwood, 2011) and F. R. Leavis (Cordner, 1991).
16 Carroll, 1996, pp. 231–237. This, of course, presupposes and/or attributes particular psychological and/or moral features to an imagined audience member. Clearly, this is not always apposite. Thus, philosopher and immoralist, Anne Eaton has stated: "I am charmed by Humbert Humbert and revere Milton's Satan" (Eaton, 2012).
17 This position is captured well by Oscar Wilde in the preface to *The Picture of Dorian Gray*: "[t]here is no such thing as a moral or an immoral book. Books are well written or badly written" (quoted by Wayne Booth, 1988, p. 382). For a more rigorous philosophical account, see the writings of art philosopher, Monroe Beardsley (Davies, 2005).
18 Jancovich, 1993.
19 Eliot, 1923.
20 Millner et al, 2015.
21 Bindman et al, 2010–2014, vols 1–5.
22 Said, 2003. Indeed, in criticising the work of Salvador Dali, George Orwell described this approach as providing a 'benefit of clergy' (Orwell, 2008, p. 210).
23 Jacobson, 1997. See also D'Arms and Jacobson, 2000.
24 Durkheim, 1965a, 1965b, pp. 872–875.
25 Julius, 2002, p. 24.
26 Bataille, 1986, Chp 5.
27 Julius, 2002, p. 34.
28 Kant, 2009.
29 Julius, 2002, p. 32.
30 Kieran, 2003, p. 72.
31 Julius, 2002, p. 49.
32 Eaton, 2012.
33 Eaton, 2012, p. 287.
34 Eaton, 2012, p. 287.
35 Eaton, 2012, p. 287.
36 Eaton, 2012, p. 287.
37 Eaton, 2012, p. 288.
38 Razinsky, 2016, p. 9.
39 Gaut, 2007, p. 50. My emphasis.
40 Gaut, 2007, p. 85.
41 Sauchelli, 2012, p. 108. My emphasis.
42 Eaton, 2012, p. 282.
43 Not all ethical properties are aesthetically relevant. Thus Gaut explains how Aesop's moral fable of the Golden Goose only has aesthetic relevance because of the way the story is conveyed or dramatised. Without this feature, it would fail to do so because without the drama, the fantastical features of the story, it would not hold our interest or "bring home the lesson of [the character's] moral stupidity" (Gaut, 2007, pp. 85–86).
44 Buckley, 2005, especially Chp 7.
45 Morley, 2016, p. 315.
46 Benjamin, 1966, p. 244.
47 Buckley, 2005, Chp 7. Hermetic Qabalah, while drawing on Jewish mysticism (or Kabbalah), refers to a Western esoteric tradition of mysticism and the occult that emerged during the late Middle Ages and Renaissance periods in Western Europe, and perhaps had its roots in ancient Greek isopsephy (Barry, 1999). On the song, 'Station to Station,' Bowie refers to Kether and Malkuth which in Kabbalistic texts symbolise respectively the material world and the divine source (Idel, 1988). On the same song, he also references infamous occultist, Aleister Crowley ('making sure white stains') (Crowley, *White Stains*, 2008) and the rays of colour that move through the Tree of Life ('Here I am, flashing no colour') (Sturzaker and Sturzaker, 1975). Bowie's interest in Qabalah precedes this period (see, for example, 'Quicksand' ('I'm closer to the Golden Dawn,

immersed in Crowley's uniform') on his 1971 *Hunky Dory* album RCA, and it is also evident on some of his subsequent work (see, for example, 'Breaking Glass' ('Don't look at the carpet, I drew something awful on it') on his 1977 *Low* album RCA). Indeed, posters of Bowie drawing the Tree of Life were used to promote the Isolar tour and appear on the back cover of his *Station to Station* album.

48 While Bowie was most intrigued by Goebbels and his use of media, he was also fasci-
    nated by Himmler's quest to rediscover the Holy Grail of Arthurian legend (Buckley,
    2005, p. 233, See also Trynka, 2011, p. 232) and he had "eulogise[d] the work of [Nazi
    architect] Albert Speer" (Trynka, 2011, p. 229).

49 Buckley, 2005, p. 233.

50 *Hunky Dory* album, 1971 RCA.

51 Garbo was the nickname of Juan Pujol Garcia, a Spanish spy and double agent for the
    British who played a key role in Operation Fortitude, which was a British military strat-
    egy designed to deceive Hitler and the German high command about the timing and
    location of Operation Overlord (D-Day) (Hesketh, 2002).

52 Pearce, 2016.

53 Crowe, 1976b. As Bowie explained to Cameron Crowe: "Everybody was convincing
    me that I was a Messiah. . . . I got hopelessly lost in that fantasy" (Crowe, 1976b). Bowie
    also alludes to Messiah worship on the song, 'We Are Hungry Men' ('Who will buy a
    drink for me, your messiah') on his 1967 *David Bowie* album Deram.

54 Carr and Shaar Murray, 1981, p. 80.

55 Buckley, 2005, p. 225.

56 Pegg, 2002, p. 297.

57 Doggett, 2011, p. 241.

58 Doggett, 2011, p. 255.

59 O'Leary, 2010b.

60 It also found support in the false allegation the Duke, on 2 May 1976, made a Nazi salute
    to fans at London's Victoria Station while standing in the back of an open-top Mercedes
    convertible (Doggett, 2011, pp. 255–256). The moment became known as the 'Heil and
    Farewell' incident on account of newspaper headlines of the time (Stewart, 1976) that
    put this particular slant on Bowie's farewell to fans before his relocation to Berlin.

61 Crowe, 1976b. In an earlier interview in Stockholm on 26 April 1976 the Duke stated:
    "I believe Britain could benefit from a fascist leader. I mean fascist in its true sense,
    not Nazi. After all, fascism is really nationalism" (Sheffield, 2016, p. 131). In both the
    Playboy and Stockholm interviews, Bowie can be viewed as engaged in method acting
    the Duke. While he distances himself from the Nazis in the Stockholm interview, and
    therefore their anti-semitism, and while he perhaps confused fascism with nationalism as
    suggested by Simon Critchley (Fosset, 2016), the Duke consistently advocated a totali-
    tarian vision.

62 Crowe, 1976b.

63 Crowe, 1976b.

64 O'Leary, 2010b.

65 Elsaesser, 2014, pp. 263–305.

66 A number of punk musicians wore swastikas in the late 1970s, perhaps most notably Sid
    Vicious of the Sex Pistols and Siouxsie Sioux of Siouxsie and the Banshees. However,
    for these artists and for many (perhaps most) punks the swastika was more a fashion
    statement and a form of inter-generational rebellion than sympathy for National Front
    politics (Morley, 2012).

67 Sheffield, 2016, p. 131.

68 Borschel-Dan, 2016.

69 While some biographers have claimed Bowie suffered from cocaine psychosis during
    the period (see, for example, Spitz, 2009), Carlos Alomar, a guitarist who worked with
    Bowie on the *Station to Station* album, noted "David was always able to manage the
    decision-making" when the album was recorded (Light, 2017).

70 Thus, at the end of the 1976 interview in Playboy Magazine, Cameron Crowe asks the Duke: "Do you believe and stand by everything you've said?" to which he replies "Everything but the inflammatory remarks" (Crowe, 1976b).

71 Het Popgebeuren, 1977.

72 Hill, 2016, pp. 77–78.

73 Hilburn, 1974.

74 O'Grady, 1975b.

75 Crowe, 1976a.

76 Indeed, as part of the Station to Station tour set, the Duke sang Bertolt Brecht and Kurt Weill's 'Alabama Song' from their 1930 opera, *Rise and Fall of the City of Mahogany*. The song provides "a savagely satirical warning of decadent times" (Morley, 2016, p. 313).

77 Foucault, 1983, p. xiii.

78 Peters, 2020.

79 Hill, 2016, p. 78.

80 'Fame' (*Young Americans* album, 1975 RCA). The song was included as part of the set on the 1976 Isolar tour.

81 Fromm, 2001.

82 Fromm, 2001, p. 3.

83 Fromm, 2001, p. 4.

84 Crowe, 1976b.

85 Buckley, 2005, p. 246.

86 Buñuel, 1984.

87 Though, unless it was faux outrage, it seemed to offend a *Daily Mirror* journalist who declared the film "distasteful and grotesque" (*Daily Mirror*, 1976, p. 15).

88 Buñuel, 1929.

89 Buckley, 2005, p. 246.

90 Gitanes have always been considered extremely cool, so cool in fact the French government considered banning them in 2016 (Cockburn, 2016).

91 Buckley, 2005, p. 247.

92 Buckley, 2005, p. 253.

93 Buckley, 2005, p. 248. Indeed, Bowie had captured the feel of this period on his 1973 *Aladdin Sane* album.

94 *Triumph of the Will* is a Nazi propaganda film covering the 1934 Nuremberg Rally. It was directed and produced by Leni Riefenstahl and released in 1935.

95 Devereaux, 1998, p. 231.

96 Buckley, 2005, p. 247.

97 Bowie would later act out the first station of the cross when he played the role of Pontious Pilate in Scorsese's controversial 1988 film, *The Last Temptation of Christ*.

98 The Tree of Life is an archetype present in many mythological, religious and/or philosophical traditions (Regardie, 2001).

99 Doggett, 2011, p. 244.

100 Doggett, 2011, p. 244.

101 *Station to Station* album, 1976 RCA. This particular lyric seems to draw, at least in part, on Shakespeare's *The Tempest* ('We are such stuff, As dreams are made on') (Shakespeare, 2008, Act 4, Scene 1).

102 Bowie relied extensively on the cut-ups writing method popularised by William S. Burroughs, especially from 1974 onwards. We will consider the impact of Burroughs' cut-ups technique on Bowie's creative output in the fourth essay in this collection.

103 Buckley, 2005, p. 246.

104 Bangs, 1975.

105 Bangs, 1976.

106 An artist's intention is only an aid in determining the attitude of an artwork. While it may assume considerable importance, an artist's claims about her artwork may be at odds with any plausible account of its attitude. She may under or over-claim or make

inconsistent claims over time. Moreover, as Gaut notes, "artists may intend to give insightful and sympathetic treatments of their characters, but only produce narrow-minded and censorious treatments of them" (2007, p. 108). Further, the character of an artist ought only to be relevant to assessment of an artwork's attitude where it bears a relationship to the artwork. Thus, if an author has written a novel about the Holocaust and she is a known anti-semite this aspect of biography may assume relevance. However, this ought not to be the case if the same author wrote a novel about the adventures of a unicorn in a magical kingdom (though see Brackmann, 2010 on Tolkien's letters likening the dwarves in his various writings to Jews). In the case of the Bowie artwork that is the subject of this essay, and in the context of controversy surrounding it, Bowie stated in the music press: "I am NOT a fascist" (Jones, 1977). Of course, his disavowal of fascism in the face of criticism by the Rock Against Racism movement and the Musician's Union (Musician's Union, 1976) might be viewed as counting for little if the attitude of his artwork is adjudged to strike a different chord.

107 Gaut, 2007, p. 34.
108 Saint Paul, 2008, 6:16.
109 'Golden Years' (*Station to Station* album, 1976 RCA).
110 'Golden Years' (*Station to Station* album, 1976 RCA).
111 'Golden Years' (*Station to Station* album, 1976 RCA).
112 *Siegfried* is the third of four music dramas constituting Wagner's *Ring*. The character Siegfried is a legendary hero of Germanic mythology (Baldwin, 2019).
113 'Station to Station' (*Station to Station* album, 1976 RCA). The lyric might also be read in terms of Crowley's emphasis on discovering one's 'true will' which exists in harmony with the cosmic will (Drury, 2012).
114 Devereaux, 1998, p. 244.
115 MacDonald, 1998.
116 The *Station to Station* album might be viewed as a kind of personal exorcism for Bowie in terms of his antipathy to the plasticity of Los Angeles, his struggle with cocaine and his immersion in hermetic Qabalah. This is perhaps most evident on the song 'Word on a Wing' which is essentially a prayer.
117 Curcio, 2020, p. 61.
118 Nietzsche, 2003, p. 146.
119 Kieran, 2003, p. 72.
120 Bowie collaborated with Eno during his Berlin years. Together they produced the so-called Berlin-trilogy of albums: *Low* (1977), *Heroes* (1977) and *Lodger* (1979).
121 Doggett, 2011, p. 245.
122 Quoted by Buckley, 2005, p. 256.
123 Devereaux, 1998, p. 248.
124 Gaut, 2007, p. 227.
125 Doggett, 2011, p. 256.
126 Bowie's performance can hardly be likened to Chaplin's in *The Great Dictator* (Chaplin, 1940).
127 Musician's Union, 1976.
128 Rook, 1976.
129 Het Popgebeuren, 1977.

Art

4

CUTTING UP THE LAWS OF WRITING

The Burroughs effect

Introduction

This essay considers the cut-ups writing method popularised by William Burroughs, whereby a written text(s) (*Hamlet*, The Bible, a telephone directory, a newspaper advertisement, information on a breakfast cereal box) is/are cut up and rearranged to create a new text. The method was introduced to Burroughs by Brion Gysin with whom he collaborated.[1] However, it has its origins in earlier practices, including those of the 1920s art movement, Dadaism. Thus, avant-garde poet, Tristan Tzara, famously pulled words out of a hat.[2] Burroughs' cut-ups method has had an enormous impact on a range of late twentieth- and early twenty-first-century artists, especially counter-cultural figures working within rock music. As well-known Burroughs scholar, Oliver Harris notes: "[William Burroughs] has fertilised an A to Z of postwar creativity, quite literally from Kathy Acker to Frank Zappa."[3]

In this essay, I will focus on one of Burroughs' more notable offspring, David Bowie, and on Burroughs' influence on Bowie's writing methods. In some ways, the beat godfather and the glitter mainman[4] could not have been more different. Burroughs, with his famous Fedora and penchant for guns, conjured up and perhaps queered once dominant ideas of masculinity, ones associated, at least in the US, with hardboiled detectives, mobsters, politicians, journos. Bowie, by contrast, was a more alien figure, waif-like and androgynous, more Jagger than Bogart. He was also lighter, at least on the surface. But then, it was not homicide that triggered Bowie's creative impulse.[5] In other ways, the two men were similar. They shared an interest in a number of intersecting themes: time travel,[6] space, sex, death, madness, science fiction, the occult. Both understood what is true in art as it is in life: stasis equals death, and both worked emphatically without a safety net. And both, at least artistically, considered "everything to be permitted."[7] That is, each trumpeted a life-affirming 'yes.' Both men wanted to get to the heart of contemporary culture

DOI: 10.4324/9781003140429-9

and in an accelerated fashion, to cut through it like a knife, as coincidence would have it an 18-inch Bowie knife.[8] Burroughs and Bowie were visionaries: provocateurs, collaborators, dedicated thieves.[9]

In drawing on Burroughs, Bowie did not change his thematic content, nor did the moment inaugurate his penchant for mixing. Bowie had always been an auteur, curator, bricoleur. But it did change his mode of delivery in an important way and this had an impact on his audience at the level of affect. Bowie had always been capable of affecting his audience, but to experience Bowie at his most transcendent is to listen to his music post-Burroughs, that is, after the encounter between Bowie and Burroughs. By encounter, I refer both to Bowie's engagement with Burroughs' work, most notably *Nova Express* and *The Wild Boys*, and to Burroughs' interview with Bowie for the rock magazine, *Rolling Stone*, in 1974.[10]

In order to consider and experience the Burroughs effect, I intend to focus on Bowie's work immediately after this encounter. My aim is to highlight how Bowie's writing underwent a transformation around this time, a transformation that, in conjunction with changes in musical composition, helped produce some of the most affecting songs in Bowie's corpus and to explain how this works. In my view, Bowie's best album is the first to draw explicitly on Burroughs' cut-ups method. Accordingly, the essay will focus on *Diamond Dogs*.[11] While the power of the album is obviously not reducible to Burroughs, containing as it does many other elements, the sense of vertigo the listener experiences, the sense of being out of kilter, of delirium, is heightened by use of cut-ups. However, before turning to consider how Bowie constructed lyrics both before and especially after Burroughs, the essay will first explain Burroughs' complex relationship to cut-ups, that is, how he conceived of the practice.

Cutting up Burroughs

Like Bowie, Burroughs was "an awful liar,"[12] an unreliable narrator, so we need to bear this in mind when thinking about what he had to say about cut-ups. That said, he appears to have understood and used cut-ups in two primary respects. First, he saw them as a practical tool for an artist to kick-start her creativity. Second, he saw them as a weapon in a struggle against linguistic control. I will elaborate in some depth this second understanding, that is, the politico-theoretical significance cut-ups had for Burroughs, but first let me explain their practical use. In practical terms, cut-ups provide a way to overcome artistic blockage. While "[y]ou cannot will spontaneity" you can, as Burroughs pointed out, "introduce the unpredictable spontaneous factor with a pair of scissors."[13] In other words, cut-ups serve to trigger ideas. Indeed, this could be their sole purpose. Thus, sometimes, once he arrived at an idea, Burroughs abandoned the cut-up materials that inspired it.[14] As he noted, the cut-up is "a very objective operation," one that might produce "a whole new idea" but then be used for "straight narrative."[15] Thus, he saw no obligation to accept random outcomes. Rather, an artist may choose to further randomise the initial cut-up text(s), add new cut-up texts, and/or interweave reassembled texts with narrative or simply write in a linear narrative or other literary style having found new direction.

Turning to the political dimension of Burroughs' cut-ups, he quite literally, through perhaps due to heroin-induced paranoia, viewed language – the word – as a virus, one that self-replicates through 'us,' its host.[16] That is, he saw it as something alien to 'us,' something through which 'we' have been colonised. In this sense, he viewed human being not as a sovereign self but as a relationship with this alien word-thing. Thus, if there is a 'we' or an 'us,' it is this parasitic relationship we bear to language. As Christopher Land has put it, "[f]or Burroughs, what we have come to understand as the human is in fact a symbiotic relationship of body and word-virus."[17] The key symptom of this virus, for Burroughs, is the 'voice inside,' what Land describes as "the compulsive drive to sub-vocalize."[18] It is this non-human internal monologue that produces a sense of internal coherence, of identity.

Burroughs' response was to wage war on the word-virus, on what he saw as a form of internal and external control. In this context, cut-ups operate as a circuit breaker, a jammer, a way to intervene in language's constitution of our "[apparent] subjective coherence and narrative continuity."[19] Burroughs does not attempt to free the human from the virus. After all, to be human is to be infected. Rather, Burroughs aimed to release, or at least to bring to our awareness, the non-viral aliens (the pre-linguistic 'us?'). What Burroughs sought to do through cut-ups was to challenge our sense of stable identity that is established through language's linear narrative structure and syntactical rules.[20] In this respect, we might view him, not as a writer but as engaged in a kind of guerrilla war with the word and, therefore, with himself. As he put it in *Nova Express*, "cut-ups are not for artistic purposes. The cut-ups are a weapon a sword. I bring not peace but pieces."[21]

While Burroughs sometimes spoke of escaping language,[22] his politics was not confined to this impossible desire. Rather, he recognised a war against the word to be unwinnable. The important thing was to wage it anyway. This is because, while we might always bear an umbilical relationship to language, he saw value in breaking down linguistic barriers that surround consciousness.[23] In this respect, cut-ups enable us to see differently, to recognise patterns and rhythms of experience that otherwise remain masked by linear narrative. Indeed, through the randomness of cuts-ups and their repetitions, all kinds of different word associations come into play, and they begin to take on altered and strange meanings both retrospectively and prospectively as time itself begins to warp.[24]

Crucially, cut-ups bring us closer to a felt reality. After all, experience "is realised as a series of interruptions and random juxtapositions. From this perspective, the cut-up provides a more realistic representation of an essentially cut-up phenomenological world."[25] In this respect, we can liken Burroughs to late modernist writers such as Eliot and Joyce.[26] Indeed, we might think of Burroughs as James Joyce on acid. While Bowie was perhaps not thinking of language as a word-virus, he did recognise that 'the wrong words make your listen.'[27] That is, in addition to their practical value in overcoming writer's block, he saw cut-ups as a way to tap into the reality of how we emotionally experience the world, that is, he recognised experience to be fragmentary. In the next section, we will consider Bowie's approach to writing prior to his encounter with Burroughs before considering in greater depth how his writing changed post-Burroughs and to what affect.

Before Burroughs: the dreamscape

From the outset, it should be recognised that while some of his early lyrics followed a clear narrative trajectory ('Can't Help Thinking About Me,'[28] 'Letter to Hermione,'[29] and 'Let Me Sleep Beside You'[30] provide some obvious examples), Bowie's writing was always influenced by the mythological, the collective unconscious. His primary access to this realm was through dreams. As he explained, "I have brilliantly Technicolor dreams. They're very, very strong . . . I suspect that dreams are an integral part of existence, with far more use for us than we've made of them."[31] Like Burroughs, Bowie was a REM machine. Indeed, many of Bowie's songs are not only dreamlike in their structure but make endless references to dreaming. 'Time' from the *Aladdin Sane* album[32] is a particularly good example: 'I had so many dreams, I had so many breakthroughs, But you, my love, were kind, but love has left you dreamless.'[33]

Thus, before Burroughs, Bowie's lyrics were most influenced by his own dreamscape and by the work of Carl Jung,[34] with which he was clearly familiar, and who he name-checks on 'Drive-in Saturday.'[35] Indeed, in his 1974 interview with Bowie, Burroughs notes their dreamlike quality, honing in, in particular, on 'Eight Line Poem' from Bowie's 1971 album, *Hunky Dory* and noting the song's lyrics to be "very reminiscent of [Eliot's] Waste Land."[36] Burroughs was not the first to see Eliot in Bowie. In 1972, after a Royal Festival Hall gig, a music journalist described Bowie's performance as "T. S. Eliot with a rock and roll beat."[37] Bowie's ability to tap into the collective unconscious was then, strong from the start whether he drew on his own dreams or (and despite his disavowals) those of others.[38] As we will see, however, Burroughs enabled Bowie to accelerate and deepen this process, while at the same time effacing himself to powerful artistic effect.

After Burroughs: accelerating the process

Bowie was capable of giving audiences a heightened experience before Burroughs, but after Burroughs, he was able to do so in a new, more direct way. Of course, Bowie had always sought to be direct. As he explained in the 1974 interview with Burroughs, he wanted to create an immediacy of experience: "Things have to hit for the moment,"[39] he insisted. The problem was one of taking too long to say it, as well as the impossibility of doing so through literal words. It is for this reason that Bowie was drawn to the image: "That's one of the reasons I'm into video, the image has to hit immediately" he explained to Burroughs.[40] Cut-ups resonated with Bowie's general approach. That is, he saw how they privileged the image over the word, how they are concerned with imagistic priority. Crucially, Bowie recognised how cut-ups help to convey the ineffable, that which cannot be captured in literal words.[41]

Indeed, this concern lay at the heart of his exploration with music more generally, one he likened to a search for God. As he put it: "[t]hey are very similar. There's an effort to reclaim the unmentionable, the unsayable, the unseeable, the unspeakable."[42] Cut-ups assist in producing this affective experience because words, which would otherwise get in the way,[43] are transformed into images which offer glimpses, flickers of sensual immediacy, something rich just out of reach. That is, Bowie understood that in the fragments we recognise the patterns and rhythms of our experience. We sense something real and are undone. Like Burroughs, Bowie wasn't particularly interested in analysing text. Commenting on *Nova Express*, he explained, he found there "a whole wonder-house of strange shapes and colors, tastes, feelings."[44] Bowie got Burroughs through the sensory landscape his writing provoked and cut-ups enabled him to deliver by way of injection.

Cut-ups also enabled Bowie to process information more quickly, "accommodating a mind that couldn't slow down."[45] Commenting on a digitalised version of the method he developed in the 1990s, Bowie explained cut-ups as akin to "a technological dream. . . [creating] images from a dream state, without having to go through the boredom of having to go to sleep . . . or get stoned."[46] They also enabled him to impose some degree of order on his own fragmented thought forms, thought forms that came dangerously close to disintegration in the mid-1970s. After all, Bowie was a reservoir of ideas and images. He could barely contain himself. Creativity poured out of him both in the sense of genius and in the sense of leakage. As he stated in 1975, "I've had to do cut-ups . . . so that I might be able to put it all back into some coherent form again."[47] The writing method also offered Bowie a way to distance himself from his words and their meaning. That is, they enabled him to sever his writing from the personal, the autobiographical, as well as from any interpretational commitments he may have had. They enabled him to "consign his deepest, darkest personal thoughts to the realms of the random and obscure."[48]

Diamond Dogs

Yet, on *Diamond Dogs*, his first post-Burroughs artistic creation, Bowie's absence, occasioned by cut-ups, vies with presence in the sense of "almost frightening levels of passion in his performance."[49] This passion, the sweep from a deep register to a soaring falsetto, which is particularly apparent on 'Sweet Thing' and 'Sweet Thing (Reprise),' speaks more eloquently than words. As Simon Critchley notes, "a world is disclosed to us . . . emotionally rather than rationally," through "the link between voice (*die Stimme*) and mood (*die Stimmung*)."[50] This triangulation of passion, music both melodic and jarring, and cut-up lyrics, so affecting in Bowie's oeuvre, come together first and best on *Diamond Dogs*.

The album creates a post-apocalyptic soundscape. Peter Doggett has described it as a "dark study in cultural disintegration."[51] It "pushe[d] past whatever rock 'n' roll had been, slashing and mutilating it before carting it off to the graveyard."[52] The album was certainly Bowie's most dystopian. It drew explicitly on George Orwell's 1984.[53] Indeed, Bowie had originally intended to present Orwell's novel in musical form. The *Dogs* album was Bowie's response to the Orwell estate's refusal to grant him the legal rights to do so. Nevertheless, Bowie plunders the novel: think of songs like 'Big Brother,' 'We are the Dead,' and, of course, with its Issac Hayes-inspired riff, '1984': "They'll split your pretty cranium, and fill it full of air, And tell you that your eighty, but brother you won't care."[54]

In many ways, *Diamond Dogs* was likely to struggle as an album given the absence of the legendary Mick Ronson, who had been key to Bowie's success to this point. Nevertheless, and despite some critics' dislike of the album,[55] Bowie managed to offer an experience of the sublime. He does so partly because of Mike Garson's incredible piano playing, "the four-note piano motif that underpins the verses," and because of "the repeated use of a cavernous bass-drum beat, and the almost visual impact of the strings."[56] One need only listen to the nine-minute triptych that lies in the middle of side one: 'Sweet Thing/Candidate/Sweet Thing (Reprise),' described by Matthew Lindsay as "an exquisitely layered . . . urban torch song."[57] In my opinion, this is not only the best part of the album but the best piece of music Bowie ever produced. These songs are highly emotional. They trade in vulnerability and longing, but also transport and delight.

'Sweet Thing' is one of my favourite Bowie songs. I love the melancholic mood. The sensitive way it explores feelings of isolation and loneliness through an imagined, perhaps real, encounter with an older sex worker. At first, it seems like an emotionless fuck as Bowie 'puts pain in a stranger,' but as the song develops so does tenderness. Through musical tone and lyrical opacity, 'Sweet Thing' produces an awareness that all in the world is not in sync with the self. In such moments, our out of kilter selves sense something more, something different, something richer. It is the arousal of this feeling which helps explain why our relationship to Bowie is one of such deep resonance. In terms of the song's lyrics, cut-ups, precluding an authoritative reading as they do, convey creative agency on the listener. And "[w]e fill in the gaps with our imagination, with our longing."[58]

Diamond Dogs creates a tension between dark and light, sinister, yet seductive. Positioned somewhere between glam rock (or in Bowie's case, art rock), soul/ funk and the soon-to-arrive punk, *Diamond Dogs* is a transitional album. Bowie was always on the move. It's not an album for purists or genre-junkies but that was never Bowie's shtick. Rather, *Diamond Dogs* is an assemblage of styles, a montage. It is symphony and cacophony. It opens with spoken word accompanied by synths ('Future Legend'), pays homage to the Rolling Stones ('Diamond Dogs')[59] and closes with the hypnotic 'Chant of the Ever Circling Skeletal Family.' In betwixt, we move from Frank Sinatra-like crooning to German composer Karl Heinz Stockhausen. When you listen to *Diamond Dogs*, it ain't just your mother who's in a whirl.

The album creates a sense of vertigo, a state through which we gain access to something sacred. However, it is not just Bowie's three octave progression that

produces a particular affective relation with the listener. Rather, the lyrics are crucial. For discordant music, and the mood it establishes, might be undermined by
common sense lyrics, one's with a linear or otherwise clear narrative structure.
Through cut-ups Bowie ensured the album remains lyrically opaque. He did so by
drawing on a collection of notebooks and diaries in which he had recorded "flashes
of inspiration" alongside "images borrowed from books [and] TV advertisements."
He even used "labels stuck on the Olympic Studios mixing consoles" where *Diamond Dogs* was recorded.[60]

As Anneliese Cooper has noted, this produces "a doubling down on meaning-
lessness,"[61] a kind of pincer movement whereby both text and sound unravel. As
they do so, dissonance and ambiguity heighten the listening experience. After all,
the fragmentation of his music and his lyrics are us. They point both to the multiplicity of who we are and who we might become. This is especially so in relation
to gender and sexuality, themes that loom large on the album. Ultimately, Bowie
captures a felt corporeal truth,[62] the truth of our inauthenticity, our dislocation, and
we feel it riff after riff.

And from the outset Burroughs is there. Think of 'Future Legend,' the first
song on the album setting the scene and mood ('And in the death, As the last
few corpses lay rotting on the slimy thoroughfare, The shutters lifted in inches in
Temperance Building, High on Poacher's Hill, And red, mutant eyes gaze down
on Hunger City'). Here, perhaps anticipating punk, Bowie's cut-ups draw on Burroughs' *The Wild Boys*, on the idea of marauding homosexual adolescents bent on
the downfall of Western civilisation. We recall the roller-skate boys who "swerve
down a wide palm-lined avenue into a screaming blizzard of machine-gun bullets,
sun glinting on their knives and helmets, lips parted eyes blazing."[63] And, of course,
those red mutant eyes that gaze down on Hunger City are hardly accidental. They
appear a decade earlier on the 1964 Calder edition of *Naked Lunch*.[64] Crucially,
however, Bowie's cut-ups complement a distorted sonic landscape. "Echo, synthe-
sised sound, vari-speed vocals and feedback" interweave with randomised words to
intensify a sense of "rotting from within."[65]

However, nothing on *Diamond Dogs* captures the "lyrical dissocia-
tion . . . [and] . . . romantic image-mongering"[66] as vividly as 'Sweet Thing/
Candidate/Sweet Thing (Reprise).' Cut-ups undermine narrative sense replacing
it with "enduring images . . . photographs . . . the couple caught in a doorway"[67]
on 'Sweet Thing,' their later hand-holding suicide in the river on 'Candidate,' and
who could forget Bowie's cocaine snowstorm on 'Reprise.'[68] As Doggett notes,
what mattered "was sound and the visions it implied, not the literal meaning of
the words. [Through cut-ups] Bowie was effectively painting with the colours of
music."[69]

Bowie continued to use cut-ups till his death. He also drew on other techniques that gestured in the same direction, including ones that applied chance
more explicitly to music construction as well as lyric writing, such as Brian Eno's
Oblique Strategies, whereby cards containing instructions were randomly distributed
to Bowie and his musicians: 'Only one element of each kind,' 'What would your

closest friend do?' 'Try faking it,' 'Honour thy error as a hidden intention,' and my favourite, 'Gardening not architecture.'[70] The last one, as well as the suggestion he play drums, annoyed guitarist, Carlos Alomar, though he subsequently used the strategy in teaching music at the Stevens Institute of Technology in New Jersey.[71] Bowie, Eno and Burroughs all shared a desire to plan accidents[72] and a recognition that boredom is "the enemy of creativity."[73]

However, as we have seen in this essay, Bowie's use of cut-ups, as well as other techniques he adopted, is not reducible to overcoming artistic blockage. Rather, they enabled him to mirror our felt fragmented realities. Like Burroughs, Bowie recognised how language distorts self-perception. But he also saw the need to bypass language in his quest to convey the ineffable. Indeed, with his 1977 *Low* album,[74] we see Bowie push further his distrust of language. Thus, in addition to his use of cut-ups, he adopted a purely instrumental approach on side 2 and, on some songs, resorted to made-up language ('Cheli venco deho, Cheli venco deho, Malio, Mmmm-mm-mm-ommm').[75] This served not only to foreground the texture, tone and mood of his voice, but also to remove his 'songs' from a linguistic interpretative framework or at least to locate them at the limits of language.[76] In my view, *Diamond Dogs* is Bowie at his best. However, I'll close with *Low* and, therefore, a shift in his musical register, though not his reliance on cut-ups: 'Share bride failing star, Care-line, Care-line, Care-line.'[77]

Conclusion

This essay has considered the influence of William Burroughs on Bowie's lyric construction and, therefore, on the overall mood and feel of his music. It focused on *Diamond Dogs*, Bowie's first post-Burroughs artistic creation. Bowie's use of cut-ups on this album and, subsequently, enabled him to accelerate his writing process. This in itself contributed to his prolificacy. It also helped him to distance himself from the personal, the autobiographical, a fact that squared with his renunciation of the idea of authenticity, a theme we considered in the second essay in this collection. Crucially, cut-ups helped Bowie to convey the ineffable, that which cannot be captured in literal words. They enabled him to exchange words for images and this served to complement a creative approach that recognised the world is disclosed to us emotionally, not rationally. With the *Dogs* album, Bowie enabled text as well as sound to unravel, thereby heightening a sense of fragmentation. As he stripped himself away, he invited us in. And once inside, we experienced personal truths and exciting possibilities care of the democratic space his use of cut-ups helped create. Through the album, we recognise 'ourselves,' or in Burroughs' terms, the non-viral aliens.

Notes

1 See, for example, Gysin and Burroughs (1960) and (1978).
2 Browning, 1979.

3 Harris, 1999, p. 243. As Harris' reference to Frank Zappa indicates, Burroughs' influence has transcended literature. Indeed, he appears to have had a particular influence on numerous counter-cultural figures within the world of rock'n' roll (Rae, 2019).
4 Copetas, 1974.
5 Burroughs claimed his killing of his second wife, Joan Vollmer, in September 1951 with a handgun led him to write. He literally had "to write his way out" from under the "ugly spirit" that haunted him (Burroughs, 1985, p. 135).
6 For Burroughs, time travel is less a theme than "the aim of the form" of his novels (Harris, 2014, p. xiii).
7 Burroughs, 1960, p. 61. While this claim is borne out by both men's endless mixing of genres and incapacity for fidelity, Bowie also paraphrases Aleister Crowley's "Do what thou wilt shall be the whole of the law" (2018)) on the song 'After all' on the *The Man Who Sold the World* album, 1970 ('Live till your rebirth and do what you will').
8 Burroughs refers to the Bowie knife in *The Wild Boys*, 1971. Bowie has explained his choice of name in terms of wanting "a truism about cutting through the lies" (Copetas, 1974).
9 Burroughs has stated: 'Everything belongs to the inspired and dedicated thief' (2013) while Bowie described himself as a 'tasteful thief' (Crowe, 1976b). In his interview with Crowe, Bowie stated humorously, "Mick Jagger . . . is scared to walk into the same room as me even thinking any new idea."
10 Copetas, 1974.
11 1974 (RCA).
12 Copetas, 1974.
13 Quoted by Casey Rae, 2019, p. 107.
14 Burroughs, 1989, p. 29.
15 Burroughs, 1989, p. 29.
16 Burroughs, 1985, p. 47. Irrespective of Burroughs' heroin use, his ideas about language as a virus have influenced key figures within social theory who have concerned themselves with questions of knowledge, power and control. In particular, Michel Foucault and Giles Deleuze have exhibited considerable interest in Burroughs' writings (Gontarski, 2020).
17 Land, 2005, p. 450.
18 Land, 2005, p. 455.
19 Land, 2005, p. 459.
20 See also Hassan, 1963; Caveney, 1998.
21 Harris, 2014, p. xx.
22 Land, 2005.
23 Burroughs, 1989.
24 At times, Burroughs appears a shamanic figure seeing in cut-ups premonitions of the future. As he famously put it, when you cut into the present "the future leaks out" (Harris, 2014, p. xiv). It is important to note here that Burroughs is not simply commenting on a text's altered temporality, one intensified by his choice of the science fiction genre. Rather, he was noting that events disclosed by the technique sometimes and subsequently appeared to happen (Burroughs, 1989). In this sense, and to quote Bowie, cut-ups could function like "a very Western tarot" (Yentob, 1975).
25 Land, 2005, p. 459. See more generally Mottram, 1977.
26 Eliot, 2002; Joyce, 2000. Indeed, Burroughs considered Eliot's, *The Waste Land* to have been "the first great cut-up collage" (Gysin and Burroughs, 1978, p. 3).
27 'Fantastic Voyage' (*Lodger* album, 1979 RCA).
28 Single with the Lower Third 1966 Pye/Warner Bros.
29 *Space Oddity* album, 1969 Philips/Mercury.
30 *The World of David Bowie* album, 1970 Decca.
31 Roberts, 1999. Bowie has stated he kept a tape recorder by his bed so that he could write it down, whenever inspiration struck (Copetas, 1974).

32 1973.
33 See also 'When I Live my Dream' (*David Bowie* album, 1967 Deram); 'An Occasional Dream' (*Space Oddity* album, 1969 Philips/Mercury); and 'Quicksand' ('Portraying Himmler's sacred realm, of dream reality') (*Hunky Dory* album, 1971 RCA).
34 Stark, 2015a.
35 Bowie refers to 'Jung the foreman' on this song (*Aladdin Sane* album, 1973 RCA).
36 Copetas, 1974.
37 Wale, 1972.
38 In his interview with Burroughs, Bowie, when asked, had claimed to have "never read [Eliot]" (Copetas, 1974). However, Claire Armistead has suggested Bowie's song, 'Eight Line Poem,' draws on Eliot's poem, 'The Hollow Men,' especially in its reference to cacti (Armistead, 2013). Whether Bowie was familiar with Eliot in 1971, he certainly was subsequently. Indeed, he put Eliot's, *The Waste Land* on his list of his top 100 books (Johnson, 2018).
39 Copetas, 1974.
40 Copetas, 1974. Bowie was as much a visual artist as he was a musician. This focus was present from the beginning and it was something he never relinquished (Cavna, 2016): "I could have been a painter, or I could have been a musician. I opted for being a musician . . . [but] my mind . . . is more in the field of a painter" (Fanning, 1997). Indeed, after the lost weekend that was his 1980s, he seriously considered retiring from his musical career in order to concentrate on his love of visual art (Fanning, 1997).
41 Levinas, 1997, p. 8.
42 BBC Archive on 4, 2016.
43 Unlike Kant, who ranked music low in a hierarchy of the arts, given his focus on their educative value (Parret, 1998), Schopenhauer and Nietzsche agreed that of all the arts, music best enabled an escape from the misery of earthly life and a glimpse of the transcendental (Schopenhauer, 2000; Nietzsche, 1993). Elsewhere, Schopenhauer insisted music is "the mightiest of the arts" and "the true universal language" (2004).
44 Copetas, 1974.
45 Lindsay, 2016.
46 Ferreira, 2013. Bowie would later use computer technology to improve and accelerate the cut-ups process (Braga, 2016).
47 Doggett, 2011, p. 201.
48 Lindsay, 2016.
49 Doggett, 2011, p. 202.
50 Critchley, 2014, p. 34. Critchley draws here on the work of Martin Heidegger (1978).
51 Quoted by Critchley, 2014, p. 69.
52 Critchley, 2014, p. 69. Indeed, the following year, Bowie would declare "rock and roll is dead . . . Its a toothless old woman" (O'Grady, 1975a).
53 Orwell, 2004.
54 Issac Hayes produced the score for the 1971 blaxploitation film, *Shaft*. This genre of films was the first to feature soundtracks of funk and soul music.
55 According to Ken Emerson *Diamond Dogs* was "Bowie's worst album in six years . . . the music exerts so little appeal that it's hard to care what it's about" (1974). See also Lester Bangs (1975).
56 Doggett, 2011, p. 198. Mike Garson worked with Bowie throughout his career commencing in 1973.
57 Lindsay, 2016.
58 Critchley, 2014, p. 144.
59 As Paul Morley has noted, the version of the Rolling Stone's Bowie offered "was warped and full of holes, almost comical." However, it remained "deadly serious" in intent, in terms of the musical direction Bowie was charting (2016, p. 280).
60 Doggett, 2011, p. 200.
61 Cooper, 2016, p. 147.

62 Critchley, 2014, p. 54.
63 Burroughs, 1971, Chp 15. In fact, in articulating how he imagined the scene, Bowie renders use of *The Wild Boys* even more explicit: "In my mind, there was no means of transport, so they were all rolling around on these roller-skates with huge wheels on them, and they squeaked because they hadn't been oiled properly. So there were these gangs of squeaking, roller-skating, vicious hoods, with Bowie knives and furs on, and they were all skinny because they hadn't eaten enough, and they all had funny-coloured hair" (Pegg, 2002, p. 63).
64 Burroughs, 1964.
65 Doggett, 2011, p. 209.
66 Doggett, 2011, p. 202.
67 Doggett, 2011, p. 202.
68 'Is it nice in your snowstorm, freezing your brain' ('Sweet Thing (Reprise)').
69 Doggett, 2011, p. 203.
70 Brian Eno, 1979. The cards were first published in 1975 with artist and collaborator, Peter Schmidt.
71 Harford, 2016. Carlos Alomar worked with Bowie on the albums, *Young Americans* (1975), *Station to Station* (1976), *Low* (1977), *Heroes* (1977), *Lodger* (1979) and *Scary Monsters* (1980), as well as on later albums including, *Outside* (1995) and *Heathen* (2002).
72 'Planned Accidents' was the working title for Bowie's 1979 *Lodger* album produced with Brian Eno.
73 Eno, 2017.
74 Bowie worked with Brian Eno during his Berlin period (1977–1979). Together they produced the so-called Berlin trilogy of albums (*Low*, 1977 RCA; *Heroes*, 1977 RCA; *Lodger*, 1979 RCA). Bowie's exploration of electronic music was influenced by Eno but also, and importantly, by German bands, Kraftwerk, Can and Neu.
75 'Warszawa' (*Low* album, 1977 RCA).
76 Wilcken, 2005, p. 14.
77 'Subterreaneans' (*Low* album 1977 RCA).

Love

5

BOWIE LOVE

Beyond law

Introduction

In this essay we will consider the idea of love. In many respects, this idea has been present, if not always made explicit, throughout this collection, and perhaps especially so in relation to discussion of the figure of the monster. Here we will consider Bowie as a philosopher of love, though not as a philosopher of the love of wisdom, philosophy's lodestone. Rather, and to use Emmanuel Levinas' phrase, Bowie is better understood as a storehouse of a "wisdom of love"[1] and, therefore, as a philosopher who grants priority to ethics (which centres otherness) over ontology (which centres self). Western philosophy has, perhaps unsurprisingly given its egocentrism, tended to neglect love[2] in favour of a preoccupation with the question of death, one's solitary relationship to an inevitable end. While Bowie had much to say about death, including his own,[3] in this essay, I will focus on what I take to be a more central theme in his work, one that sets itself against the law, love. In linking Bowie with love, the essay is not interested in his romantic involvements,[4] albeit these often revealed a high degree of curiosity and openness in the face of difference.[5] Rather, the Bowie-love nexus to be considered concerns itself with *agape*, a Greco-Christian idea capturing the idea of a love for humanity, a universal and unconditional love or at least a striving toward it. While it need not bear a theological meaning, in the Christian sense it refers to the love of God or Christ for humankind.[6]

Given Bowie's well-known interest in Nietzsche,[7] an appeal to the idea of *agape* might seem misplaced. After all, Nietzsche viewed *agape* as Christianity's corruption and repudiation of life itself, as a "deadly war [waged] against [the] higher type of man."[8] However, and while Bowie might be viewed as an artistic exemplar of this Nietzschean figure, a heralding of the overman or superman ('You've gotta make way for the homo superior')[9] is ultimately peripheral to his art and music.

DOI: 10.4324/9781003140429-11

While he shared Nietzsche's desire to affirm life and human creativity, as well as his perspectivism[10] and antipathy toward a herd mentality,[11] it is self-effacement that lies at the centre of Bowie's corpus. It is his paring back of self, and therefore, the other-directed nature of his artistic fecundity, that renders him a useful vehicle for exploring the idea of *agape*. For as Max Scheler notes, *agape* is a love that opens human beings to the world, to what is other and, therefore, to a "superabundant vitality."[12]

Bowie love is a going beyond oneself, to ever richer meaning through community and connection. It does not involve Nietzsche's elitist, self-loving 'higher man' who, in his solitude, remains indifferent to others and to their suffering. On the contrary, and in this latter respect, Bowie has more in common with the spirit of the New Testament than Nietzsche's antichrist. Like Jesus, he cries, "I am with you always"[13] or more poetically, 'Oh no love, you're not alone . . . Gimme your hands cause you're wonderful, Oh gimme your hands.'[14] Thus, Bowie love is not Nietzsche's 'tough love.'[15] While it is not an easy thing, as we will see, it does not view compassion, something Nietzsche viewed as more dangerous than any vice,[16] to be antithetical to the creative spirit. Nor is it a matter of self-reverence,[17] and it is certainly not about assuming the place of God. That is, Bowie does not advance an 'ethics of self-deification."[18] Indeed, as we will see, Bowie rejected the idea of man-God as heathen, as a thoroughly wrong turn. Ultimately, while Nietzsche viewed suspension of the "instinct of self-preservation" to be "calamitous," a "fatality,"[19] Bowie squandered himself, time and again, in over-flowing other-directed creativity.

While *agape* might suggest the divine, and while some of Bowie's music and art can be understood as a dialogue with God, the Bowie-love nexus to be developed here remains an earthly affair. While it begins from the premise "[o]ne cannot love anybody without turning away from oneself,"[20] it focuses not on the couple, Alain Badiou's "the two,"[21] but rather is a love that radiates out. However, it does involve foregrounding Badiou's distinction between identity and difference.[22] For like Badiou, Bowie sought to privilege difference over identity, mobile otherness over static selfhood, love over law. As Badiou has explained:

> love's main enemy, the one [that must be] defeat[ed], is not the other, it is myself, the 'myself' that prefers identity to difference, that prefers to impose its world against the world re-constructed through the filter of difference.[23]

David Bowie always reconstructed the world through the filter of difference, not the difference of a specific love object (the beloved) but through difference at large. It is through these reconstructed worlds of sound and vision that he established affective relationships with fans. However, it is not the love of Bowie for fans, or indeed the love of fans for Bowie, with which we are concerned. Rather, it is the idea of love inherent in Bowie's work that is our object. Through his music, lyrics and performances, Bowie embraced an idea of love, one we might describe as *agape*, but certainly one that centres difference and offered it to fans as a choice.

This love speaks to the freedom to become, to develop, to ch-ch-change, and of course to disappoint (for loss is always a part and consequence of love). In other words, the love Bowie fostered is founded on embracing freedom to be different and on embracing the warm impermanence of the manifestation of differences in oneself and others.

Freedom here is used in the Foucauldian sense as it assumes "the possibility of being otherwise."[24] To this end, Bowie transports us from imagined necessity to a world of human, and posthuman, possibilities.[25] That is, through otherworldly constructions, and through showing us their seams, Bowie demystified the world, teased the ideological out into the open. As he stated in 1999, "I embrace the idea that there's a demystification process going on between the artist and the audience."[26] It is the ideological, the social norms we have internalised, ones that insufficiently value difference, that hold us back, that make the possibility of love recede. And it is to the undoing of these social norms, which parade as necessity, that Bowie directed his art. In this sense, Bowie's art addresses the very ground of and interconnection between love and freedom.

Further, and while transgression may be one of the modes through which social norms are challenged, it is not law breaking as such that is key for Bowie. Rather, it is the undermining of law, the order of things, the socially and cul-turally taken-for-granted, that proves crucial. To that end, Bowie preferred the parodic, the absurd, to the oppositional 'fuck you' politics of, for example, punk. As Richard Fitch has observed, he created worlds where "all social norms and rules have been suspended."[27] In doing so, he provided glimpses of possible futures and a portal onto the love necessary to realise them. In developing these ideas, this essay will focus first on Bowie's subversion of social norms as a precondition of love/freedom. It will then turn to consider three important lessons evident in Bowie's work, one's that speak to love: love as letting go, love as humility and love as posthuman.

Escaping necessity

As philosopher, Simon Critchley has noted, "Bowie's music is about yearning," and ultimately it is a yearning "for love."[28] It is Bowie's yearning for love that touches us, speaks to us the most profoundly. It disarms as it disorientates. It makes us aware of our own deep longing for transcendence of self and connection with oth-ers, for the creation of spaces "large enough for love to enter."[29] These yearnings, which pre-exist Bowie, are drawn to the surface through his music and art. Moreo-ver, through Bowie, through the worlds he describes and inhabits, they become attached to possible presents and futures. That is, Bowie enlarges our worlds. While our understanding of our world, our place in it, our life possibilities are inextricably tied up with ideology, its internalisation, its affective concretisation through/in us, Bowie breaks the spell. And because spectacular capitalism always recuperates sub-versive acts,[30] the thin white magician must always stay a step ahead, hence Bowie's endlessly playful reinventions.

An ethic of love is implicit in such activity as demystification lays the ground for human flourishing, it enables freedom to take shape. And the strange worlds Bowie conjured up brought the non-inevitability of the ordinary, the everyday, into sharp relief. His music and art helped release us from necessity, that is, from social expectations that appear natural,[31] ones which can be experienced as prosaic, and at times deadening. He enabled us to entertain new and rich possibilities. Where there had been inevitability, he foregrounded contingency and, in the process, made us conscious of (constrained though it may be) choice.

Moreover, Bowie did not project "an idealized future community."[32] Rather, as Amedeo D'Adamo notes, his "sense of the possible hinged on the way each persona was crafted and performed as an alien, foreign other who had no link to our own social background."[33] In this way, he dramatised the difference between the mundane actual and the extraordinary possible, while simultaneously refusing to rule out future communities or individual forms of becoming. Through his characters, and the landscapes they inhabited, Bowie "triggered an existential revelation in some fans,"[34] especially those who realised "[l]ove is always the possibility of being present at the birth of [a] world."[35] It is this opening of a crack in the sky that helps explain why Bowie remains such an enduring presence in many fans' lives.

Love as letting go

Loving others involves loving them in flux. In other words, it requires embracing change, their process of becoming. This, of course, can be painful. It is a lesson Bowie would give time and again through killing off objects of fan love. While rock stars, like the Who's Pete Townshend, confined auto-destructive art[36] to smashing up guitars on stage,[37] Bowie, with much less fanfare, and usually in the very moment of musical and artistic triumph, always turned it on himself. That is, he committed serial ritual suicide. He set the template for doing so with his proto-punk character, Ziggy.[38] Having killed the "Kabuki monster,"[39] he then repeated this move with a series of subsequent characters. Like a Gustav Metzger acid painting, Bowie dissolved before our eyes, only to be reconstituted elsewhere. Through the metaphorical killing of selves, Bowie chose difference over identity, over the cult of repetition (of modern pop/rock) against which Badiou warns.[40]

To be a Bowie fan then is to mourn, to let go and to learn to love again, and to become increasingly aware that this process will be repeated without end. Moreover, through his symbolic practices of death and rebirth, Bowie undercut the notion of rock and rock communities as static and repetitive. In keeping the faith, fans had not only to be willing to reconnect with Bowie but also with a Bowie community to come,[41] one that would rise like a phoenix from his ashes. Through his protean, life-affirming exercises in renewal, Bowie dramatised the fleeting quality of attachment, his take-away message being to embrace impermanence warmly. Or, to put it another way, he encouraged us to accept change in others/ourselves, in their/our life journeys, as a precondition of love, and to do so as an act of faith, for we can never truly know the other.[42] This is not an easy thing of course. In the musical context, one thinks immediately of the cries of 'Judas,' Bob Dylan faced at Manchester's Free Trade Hall in 1966 when he exchanged acoustic for electric guitar.[43] Bowie encountered this problem less due to the rapidity of his changes, but change is always unsettling for most fans and lovers. Bowie, through his characters and music, encourages us to embrace this change and the pain it necessarily entails, though he offered the consolation that the journey would never be dull.[44] In other words, Bowie alludes to the fact love is a risk but that without risk, there can be no love. And the risk we must take is to let go, to let go of ourselves and others, again and again. In this regard, Bowie love requires us to abandon fixed ideas about ourselves and others and to embrace our/their vulnerability in the service of what may come. It is a love that requires patience, duration and commitment, a love that affords us 'a different [and better] way of lasting in life.'[45]

Love as humility

The effacement of self, a reigning in of the ego, is also apparent in Bowie's fore-grounding of humility. In a Christian religious sense, humility means recognition of the self in its relation to God.[46] In a non-religious sense, it signifies an unselfing, a shedding, a paring back of self. For the purposes of this essay, we will focus on two interrelated ways that humility comes to the fore in Bowie's work. First, we will consider Bowie's ambivalent relationship with organised religion, especially Christianity. Second, we will consider, via the *Heathen* album, his concerns regarding the hubris of men. Bowie's interest in religion (Tibetan Buddhism,[47] Christianity, Judaism) and his spiritual quest more generally (Gnosticism, Kabbalism and other forms of mysticism), a searching for some kind of metaconnection, appears to have been present from the beginning. We encounter it first on 'Silly Boy Blue,' with its reference to the Tibetan 'Mountains of Lhasa'[48] and on 'Karma Man.'[49] On the song, 'The Supermen,' he alludes to the tragic nature of omnipotence, to the inability of the Gods to call time on their own lives, ('wondrous beings chained to life'/'so softly a supergod cries').[50] And on 'Quicksand,' he references occultist, Aleister Crowley ('I'm closer to the Golden Dawn, Immersed in Crowley's uniform'),[51] and later on 'Station to Station,' Hermetic Qabalah ('Here are we, one magical movement, From Kether to Malkuth').[52]

Christianity, in particular, proves to be a recurring theme in Bowie's work, and it is in relation to Christianity that we see an attraction–repulsion dynamic most at play. Thus, we can contrast the persistent and intimate prayer-like quality of some of Bowie's lyrics ('Lord I kneel before you, My word on a wing, And I'm trying hard to fit among, Your scheme of things'[53]/'All my trials Lord, Will be remembered'/[54]'Show me all you are, Open up your heart to me, And I would be your slave')[55] with his cynicism regarding the actual practices of the holy church. We witness the latter first perhaps on the song 'Five Years' where we are introduced to the cop who 'knelt and kissed the feet of the priest' and to 'the queer [who] threw up at the sight of that.'[56] This theme is again in evidence on the song 'Loving the Alien,' the alien being a metaphor for God. Here Bowie's subject is the crusades

('The Templars and the Saracens')[57] and "the political savagery implicit in claims to Christian faith"[58] or as Bowie's puts it, 'believing the strangest things, loving the alien.' More recently, on the accompanying video to the song, 'The Next Day,'[59] Bowie presents a decadent and corrupted priesthood ('they can work with satan while they dress like saints'). As Critchley has noted, Bowie's obsession with and opposition to the Christian church appears to be founded on the view that it has "fraudulently co-opted, branded, marketed and moralized the experience of transcendence."[60] It is against this arrogance of the church that Bowie railed, against the hierarchy and power that get in the way of the spiritual and, therefore, love. In the face of its eviscerating laws, Bowie demands, 'give me your freedom of spirit.'[61]

It is this desire for spirit, for affirmation of life, that drove Bowie's music and art, and that explains his endless searching for connection. As he stated, "[q]uestioning my spiritual life has always been germane to what I was writing. Always. It's because I'm not quite an atheist and it worries me."[62] In other words, while he was full of doubts, Bowie appears to have kept the God question open ('I don't pretend faith never works').[63] Importantly, however, whether Bowie's work was directed toward the big Other and/or only to others (the likes of us), it reached out. While other rock stars sought to confess/to foreground their ontology, Bowie, as we saw in the second essay in this collection, sought to commune/to establish ethical relations with fans. In doing so, he recognised, with or without God, the enduring importance of humility to love.

Moreover, Bowie's call for greater love-directed humility led him to having more than organised religion in his sights.[64] He also railed against contemporary man, against his abandonment of humility. This is one of the reasons Critchley has claimed Bowie "at times resembles an iconoclastic Lutheran."[65] This concern perhaps receives its clearest expression on the 2002 *Heathen* album. As he explained, he used the term *Heathen* as "an address from a man to life, not from man to a God, but to life itself."[66] Elsewhere, he explained the term referred to the "unilluminated mind," to:

> somebody who has lowered his standards, spiritually, intellectually, morally . . . someone who's not even bothered searching for a spiritual life anymore, who completely exists on a materialistic plain.[67]

Bowie's *Heathen* then refers to those who have substituted "the God who has died" with themselves,[68] those who have embraced the ordinary or banal, those who scream 'I don't want knowledge, I want certainty.'[69] Thus, Bowie's *Heathen* is not only hubristic but also materially consumptive and happiness directed.[70] In musical terms, think Coldplay,[71] Ed Sheeran or "the dreadful [dreadful] Bono."[72] In the face of such profanity, Bowie yearns for connection, for love: 'Ain't there one damn song that can make me break down and cry?'[73] And, of course, we yearn with him. Bowie always strikes this chord. Thus, in Berlin, when Bowie introduced the song, *Heathen*[74] with the following heartfelt plea: "God bless us. PLEASE, God bless us,"[75] he was not literally referring to a God. Rather, he was speaking to outsiders with whom he identified and who identify with him and expressing the hope that *we* are not *Heathen*. That is, he was inviting us to move beyond our ego-centred selves, in the service of a love realisable only through an embrace of difference. That is, like Badiou, Bowie recognised love to be an "opportunity . . . to enjoy a positive, creative, affirmative experience of difference."[76] Bowie's emphasis on humility, his privileging of otherness over self, comes through in his work generally though it is perhaps rendered most explicit near his end when he sings: 'seeing more and feeling less, saying no but meaning yes, this is all I ever meant, that's the message that I sent.'[77] With these loving and parting words, Bowie appears to allude to a self receding from view ('feeling less') and to otherness coming into ever sharper relief ('seeing more').

Love as posthuman

In developing the idea of *agape*, of unconditional love, Bowie's privileging of ethics (which centres otherness) over ontology (which centres self) can also be seen in his embrace of the posthuman. Posthumanism offers a critique of humanism, its underlying assumptions and limits. It recognises our imperfectability[78] and embraces our manifestation through difference. Rather than thinking about the posthuman as a loss of cognitive and moral self-mastery, as humanism does, Rosi Bradiotti argues, it enables us to understand the fluidity and multiplicity of our identities.[79] More than that, as Donna Haraway argues, it emphasises that it is our "affinity, not identity" that matters most.[80]

As long ago as 1976, Bowie declared he had "always had a repulsive desire to be something more than human."[81] Once again, as we so often do with Bowie in his twenties, we hear the voice of Nietzsche. However, Bowie's desire to move beyond human should not be understood as a desire to assume the place of God, a desire Bowie eschewed, especially in his later work, as we have already seen. Rather, Bowie's desire for 'something more' is a desire to escape the monotonous, the mundane, a desire he pursued through a series of constructions and their subsequent undoings. In other words, Bowie's trajectory is one of shedding, of self-effacement, and, therefore, a trajectory that foregrounds humility.

Bowie tried to capture this sense of 'something more,' something beyond, in various ways through his characters, music and art. He also did so through films, performing roles that were not human or only partly so. We recall, for example, Thomas Jerome Newton (*The Man Who Fell to Earth*), John Merrick (the *Elephant Man*) and John Blaylock (the vampire Bowie played in *The Hunger*). Further, through different kinds of studio processing techniques, Bowie masked the human element of his voice in order to create a sense of a sonic beyond. As Kevin Holm-Hudson has pointed out, Bowie's voice sometimes became "a sampled element in the electronic texture, divorcing it from the physical body sound-source."[82]

In this section of the essay, I will take up the theme of posthumanism through Bowie's playfulness with the theme of human/animal hybridity. This theme, which pulls at the seams of the human in a particular way, is perhaps first rendered apparent through his 1971 Egyptian Sphinx photo shoot with Brian Ward,[83] where Bowie posed as half-man, half-lion. However, this theme comes to the fore most starkly through his 1974 *Diamond Dogs* gatefold album cover, designed by photo realist Belgian artist, Guy Peellaert.[84] On the cover, Bowie appears as half-man, half-dog. The original version showed full genitalia but was later air-brushed for mass release. The airbrushed version, however, served only to neuter the creature,[85] thereby producing a crisis of sex as well as species. Indeed, the figure of the dog-man calls into question a third domain, the temporal/spiritual, given the symbol of the dog, at least in the medieval and early modern periods, referred to the devil.[86] The cover image, which might be viewed as offering a contemporary take on the early sixteenth-century monster of Ravenna,[87] is striking. Behind Bowie, squat two human, perhaps demonic, bitches.[88] While they might be described as grotesque,[89] it is more difficult to characterise Bowie in this way. Certainly, his intense fixed gaze, his knowingness, is unlikely to illicit pity. Rather, he appears powerful and defiant, delighting in the celebration of hybridity, in being one of 'the strangest living curiosities,' as the accompanying text declares. If there is disgust, there is also recognition and desire.

The image on the *Diamond Dogs* cover points to a (perhaps *the*) central taboo in Western culture: thou shall not mix species, which, of course, is a prohibition against bestiality. The image is provocative, however, not primarily because of bestial possibilities, but because it serves to remind us of our inability to distinguish between human and animal, that is, it points to our own animality. The distinction between human and animal has been important in defining the contours of humanity, in rendering us human. Yet, anxiety concerning the distinction is long-standing. According to Joyce Salisbury, it can, in the West, be dated to the late Middle Ages.[90] Anxiety over perceived porousness between human and animal became more pronounced with the passage of time and the discomforting findings of science.[91] Certainly, by the end of the eighteenth century, the Western worldview, resting on the idea of the "Great Chain of Being," was under enormous pressure from the scientific community.[92] And, as Donna Haraway notes, by the end of the twentieth century: "the boundary between human and animal [was] thoroughly breached."[93] The specialness of *homo sapiens* at the biological level has become even more suspect since the findings of the Human Genome Project[94] which push an already fragile idea of human close to breaking point.

And yet, in the face of this crisis of the 'human,' we should not be alarmed. The human was always already a construct that divided us not only from other species but from each other and ourselves. Behind the lie of ontological purity, whose logical end is always disturbing and sometimes leads to the death camp, lies the beautiful truth of hybridity. Metaphorically and artistically, Bowie points the way. In the face of taboo, the royal 'No,' he always seemed to say 'Yes.' Yes, to difference, yes, to mixture, yes, to connection. As Critchley notes, what Bowie seemed to offer was "an absolute and unconditional affirmation of life in all of its chaotic complexity, but also its moments of transport and delight."[95] And, after all, if we can embrace the hybrid, the monster, the posthuman, do we not guarantee the liveability and loveability of every life? Bowie love or his ethical relation to difference might be expressed in Judith Butler's terms as a refusal "to foreclose the challenge . . . difference delivers."[96] Like Butler, Bowie invites us:

> to learn to live in the anxiety of that challenge, to feel the surety of one's epistemological and ontological anchor go, but be willing, in the name of the human to become something other than what it is traditionally assumed to be.[97]

Conclusion

This essay has, through Bowie, considered the theme of love as *agape*. It is an important, indeed central theme cascading through his work. Crucially, Bowie love lies in an ethical relation, one that prioritises the other over the self. Bowie explored otherness through an engagement that required him to pare back himself. As Critchley, quoting Anne Carson,[98] has noted, "[l]ove dares the self to leave itself behind" in order "that something new can come into being."[99] In proceeding in this way, Bowie constituted the ground for an ethical freedom for himself and others. After all, as Foucault has noted, "ethics is the considered form that freedom takes when it is informed by reflection."[100] And, of course, proper reflection leads one to difference, to the other, and therefore to love.[101] In other words, in the face of difference, what ultimately rings out in Bowie's work is a resounding 'Yes.' As Critchley puts it: "his music yearned for and allowed us to imagine . . . new forms of being together, new intensities of desire and love in keener visions and sharper sounds."[102] Amen.

Notes

1 Beals, 2007. See also Alain Badiou, 2012.
2 Notable philosophers who have addressed the idea of love favourably include Soren Kirkegaard (2009), Emmanuel Levinas (1999) and Alain Badiou, 2012.
3 See, for example, 'My Death waits like a Bible truth' ('My Death' by Jacques Brel performed by Bowie on the Ziggy Stardust tour 1972), 'I'm frightened by the total goal' ('Quicksand' *Hunky Dory* album, 1971 RCA), 'Time, he's waiting in the wings' ('Time' *Aladdin Sane* album, 1973 RCA), 'When the kingdom comes' ('Kingdom Comes' (*Scary Monsters* album, 1980 RCA)), 'Here I am not quite dying' ('The Next day' (*The Next Day* album, 2013 ISO/Columbia)), 'Look up here, I'm in Heaven' ('Lazarus' (*Blackstar* album, 2016 ISO/Columbia/Sony)). On Bowie and death, see Stark, 2015b; Potter and Cobb, 2016.
4 Leigh, 2014.
5 Thus Bowie had sexual and romantic relationships with men and women who identified as straight, gay, bisexual and/or transgender (Kohn, 2016).
6 Outka, 1977.
7 This interest is most apparent on his early albums, particularly *The Man Who Sold the World* (1970) and *Hunky Dory* (1971).
8 Nietzsche, 1976b, p. 571.
9 'Oh, You Pretty Things' (*Hunky Dory* album, 1971 RCA).

10 Perspectivism is a philosophical tradition denying the idea of absolute truths (Nietzsche, 2003). For discussion of Nietzsche's perspectivism, see Danto, 1965; Schacht, 1983; Nehamas, 1985; Richardson, 1996.

11 Watts, 1972; Shaar Murray, 1977.

12 Scheler, 1971, p. 192.

13 Saint Matthew 28:20 (2008).

14 'Rock 'n' Roll Suicide' (*The Rise and fall of Ziggy Stardust and the Spiders from Mars* album, 1972 RCA).

15 As Martha Nussbaum has noted, Zarathustra's journey ends when he jettison's pity (1994, p. 152). Indeed, a critique of compassion is, as Michael Fraser notes, "one of the central themes, if not the central theme, in Nietzsche's immoralist ethics" (Fraser, 2006, p. 49).

16 Nietzsche, 1968. Elsewhere Nietzsche states that compassion "preserves what is ripe for destruction, it defends those who have been disinherited and condemned by life" (Nietzsche, 1976b, p. 573).

17 Nietzsche, 2003.

18 Berkowitz, 1996, p. 150.

19 Nietzsche, 1976a, p. 548.

20 Scheler, 1971, p. 198.

21 Badiou, 2012, p. 28.

22 Badiou, 2012, p. 22.

23 Badiou, 2012, p. 60.

24 Foucault, 1988a, p. 154.

25 D'Adamo, 2019.

26 Paxman, 1999.

27 Fitch, 2015, p. 29.

28 Murphy, 2014.

29 Critchley, 2012, p. 152.

30 Debord, 1994, p. 102.

31 D'Adamo, 2019, p. 2.

32 D'Adamo, 2019, p. 8.

33 D'Adamo, 2019, p. 8.

34 D'Adamo, 2019, p. 9.

35 Badiou, 2012, p. 26.

36 Auto-destructive art is a term invented by artist, Gustav Metzger (1999).

37 Critchley, 2014, pp. 115–116.

38 Bowie famously announced the death of Ziggy at Hammersmith Odeon on 3 July 1973 ('Not only is it the last show of the tour, but its the last show that we'll ever do'). He followed this statement with the song 'Rock 'n' Roll Suicide' (*The Rise and fall of Ziggy Stardust and the Spiders from Mars* album, 1972 RCA).

39 Buckley, 2005, p. 146.

40 Badiou, 2012, p. 98.

41 Ketcham, 2016, p. 178.

42 Derrida, 2005, p. 54.

43 Fleming, 2016.

44 "I don't know where I'm going from here, but I promise it won't be boring," Madison Square Gardens concert, 8 January 1997 (Blair, 2016).

45 Badiou, 2012, p. 33.

46 Herbermann, 2010.

47 Muchall, 2016.

48 *David Bowie* album, 1967 Deram.

49 *The World of David Bowie* album, 1970 Decca. See Muchall, 2016.

50 *The Man Who Sold the World* album, 1970 Mercury.

51 *Hunky Dory* album, 1971 RCA. See Regardie, 2015.

52 *Station to Station* album, 1976 RCA. On Hermetic Qabalah, see footnote 47 in the third essay in this collection.

53 'Word on a Wing' (*Station to Station* album, 1976 RCA).

54 'Sunday' (*Heathen* album, 2002 ISO/Columbia).

55 'I would be Your Slave' (*Heathen* album, 2002 ISO/Columbia).

56 *The Rise and Fall of Ziggy Stardust and the Spiders from Mars* album, 1972 RCA.

57 *Tonight* album, 1984 EMI.

58 Critchley, 2014, p. 165.

59 *The Next Day* album, 2013 ISO/Columbia.

60 Critchley, 2014, p. 166.

61 'Sex and the Church' (*The Buddha of Suburbia* album, 1993 Virgin/EMI).

62 DeCurtis, 2003.

63 'Bus Stop' (*Tin Machine* album, 1989 EMI).

64 Bowie has stated that he has "no empathy for organised religion" (Cavanagh, 1997, p. 52). And, in an interview with Maria Karchilaki for Greek Television, he stated, in response to a question as to whether he was religious, "I'm probably the least religious person you've met" (Karchilaki, 2002)

65 Critchley, 2014, p. 167.

66 Karchilaki, 2002.

67 O'Leary, 2014.

68 Critchley, 2014, p. 157. Here Critchley is referencing Nietzsche's famous pronouncement in the *Gay Science* (Nietzsche, 2019). Indeed, Bowie had expressed concerns of this kind as early as 1972: "We'll all go to hell cause we set ourselves up as gods" (quoted by Mick Rock, 2001).

69 'Law (Earthlings on Fire)' (*Earthling* album, 1997 Arista/Virgin).

70 The banal pursuit of happiness has become increasingly ubiquitous and mandated institutionally and by the market (see Bruckner, 2011).

71 Bowie famously turned down the 'opportunity' to work with *Coldplay* when they invited him to perform with them one of their songs (Tan, 2016).

72 Critchley, 2014, p. 100.

73 'Young Americans' (*Young Americans* album, 1975 RCA).

74 *Heathen* album, 2002 ISO/Columbia.

75 Bowie, 2002. The concert took place at the Max-Schmeling-Halle on 22/9/02.

76 Badiou, 2012, p. 66.

77 'I Can't Give Everything Away' (*Blackstar* album, 2016 ISO/Columbia/Sony).

78 Braidotti, 2000, p. 158.

79 Braidotti, 2013.

80 Haraway, 1985, p. 71. Haraway does not use the term posthuman explicitly. Rather, through her figure of the *Cyborg* "she calls into question three key boundaries that have helped preserve the sanctity of 'the human' as a self contained being" (Gane, 2005, p. 431). These boundaries are: human/animal; animal-human/machine; and physical/nonphysical (Haraway, 1985, pp. 68–69).

81 Crowe, 1976a.

82 Kevin Holm-Hudson, 2018, p. 214.

83 Bowie initially considered this image for the cover of the *Hunky Dory* album, but later abandoned it (Pegg, 2002, p. 348).

84 The *Diamond Dogs* cover image, which Bowie story boarded, was initially conceived through Terry O'Neill's photo shoot of Bowie with a Great Dane.

85 Redmond, 2013, p. 381.

86 Rowland, 1974, p. 26.

87 The Monster of Ravenna 'appeared' in 1512 near the Italian city of Ravenna. It was depicted as male-headed with breasts, birds wings and feet, and a devil's horn protruding from its head (Paré, 1982, p. 6).

88 These two figures, apparently, were based on the Coney Island Cavalcade Variety Show performers, Alzoria Lewis (aka 'the Turtle Girl') and Johanna Dickens (aka 'the Bear Girl') (see Cann, 2010, p. 325).

89 Bakhtin, 1984.

90 Salisbury, 1994, p. 2.

91 Thomas, 1983, p. 122.

92 According to this view, the world was believed to be ordered and hierarchical. God sat at the apex, below him sat the angels, then human beings, followed by various classes of non-human animals, and finally other lesser living matter (see Lovejoy, 1970).

93 Haraway, 1985, p. 68.

94 Most significantly, while 'human beings might share 99.9% commonality at the genetic level, there is nothing as yet identifiable as absolutely common to all human beings. That is, there is no genetic lowest common denominator, no genetic essence' (Robert and Baylis, 2003, p. 4).

95 Critchley, 2016, p. 170. This book is an updated version of Critchley's 2014 *Bowie*, written after Bowie's death and the release of his final album, *Blackstar*.

96 Butler, 2004, p. 35.

97 Butler, 2004.

98 Carson, 2005, p. 162.

99 Critchley, 2012, p. 152.

100 Foucault, 1997, p. 284.

101 Of course, for Foucault, concern for the other is to be realised through 'care of the self.' As he notes, "care for the self is ethical in itself; but it implies complex relationships with others insofar as this *ethos* of freedom is also a way of caring for others" (Foucault, 1997, p. 287). However, in this essay, Bowie love has been presented as other-directed in a much stronger sense. It is a self-effacing love, one that has more in common with New Testament Christianity, than ancient Greek thought.

102 Critchley, 2016, p. 173.

REFERENCES

Adorno, Theodor, *In Search of Wagner (1966)* (London: Verso, 2005).

Ammon, Theodore G. (ed), *David Bowie and Philosophy: Rebel Rebel* (Chicago: Open Court, 2016).

Anttonen, Veikko, 'Sacred' in Willi Braun and Russell T. McCutcheon (eds) *Guide to the Study of Religion* (London: Cassell, 2000).

Armistead, Claire, 'Did David Bowie Pinch a Cactus from TS Eliot?' *The Guardian* 21/3/2013 www.theguardian.com/books/booksblog/2013/mar/21/did-david-bowie-steal-from-ts-eliot (last accessed: 1/12/2020).

Attali, Jacques, *Noise: The Political Economy of Music* (Minneapolis: University of Minnesota Press, 1985).

Atwood, Sara, *Ruskin's Educational Ideas* (Aldershot: Ashgate, 2011).

Auslander, Philip, *Performing Glam Rock: Gender and Theatricality in Popular Music* (Ann Arbor, MI: University of Michigan Press, 2006).

Badiou, Alain, *In Praise of Love* (London: Serpents Tail, 2012).

Baker, David, 'Bowie's Covers: The Artist as Modernist' in Toija Cinque, Christopher Moore and Sean Redmond (eds) *Enchanting David Bowie: Space Time Body Memory* (London: Bloomsbury, 2015) pp. 103–118.

Bakhtin, Mikhail, *Rabelais and His World (1965)* (London: John Wiley & Sons, 1984).

Baldwin, James, *The Story of Siegfried* (Frankfurt: Outlook Verlag, 2019).

Bangs, Lester, 'Johny Ray's Better Whirlpool' *Creem* 1/1975 www.bowiegoldenyears.com/press/75-01-00-creem.html (last accessed: 1/12/2020).

Bangs, Lester, 'Chickenhead Comes Home to Roost' *Creem* 4/1976, Brian Eno's webpage www.moredarkthanshark.org/eno_int_creem-apr76b.html (last accessed: 1/12/2020).

Barry, Kieran, *The Greek Qabalah: Alphabetic Mysticism and Numerology in the Ancient World* (York Beach, ME: Samuel Weiser, Inc, 1999).

Barthes, Roland, 'The Death of the Author' in Stephen Heath (ed) *Image, Music, Text* (London: Fontana, 1967).

Bass, Jacquelynn, *Marcel Duchamp and the Art of Life* (Cambridge, MA: MIT Press, 2019).

Bataille, Georges, *Eroticism: Death and Sensuality (1962)* (San Francisco, CA: City Lights Books, 1986).

Bauman, Zygmunt, *Postmodern Ethics* (Oxford: Blackwell, 1993).

BBC Archive on 4, 'David Bowie: Verbatim' (30/1/2016) www.bbc.co.uk/sounds/play/b06z5pts (last accessed: 1/12/2020).

Beals, Corey, *Levinas and the Wisdom of Love: The Question of Invisibility* (Waco, TX: Baylor University Press, 2007).

Benjamin, Walter, 'Art in the Age of Mechanical Reproduction' in *Reflections: Essays, Aphorisms, Autobiographical Writings* (New York: Harcourt Brace Jovanovich, 1966).

Berkowitz, Peter, *Nietzsche: The Ethics of an Immoralist* (Cambridge, MA: Harvard University Press, 1996).

Bindman, David et al *Image of the Black in Western Art* vol 1–5 (Cambridge, MA: Harvard University Press, 2010–2014).

Blackstone, William, *Commentaries on the Laws of England 1765–1769* vol 1–4 (Chicago: University of Chicago Press, 1979).

Blair, Olivia, 'David Bowie: "The Iconic Singer's Most Profound Quotes",' *The Independent* 11/1/2016 www.independent.co.uk/news/people/david-bowie-the-best-quotes-from-the-starman-a6805536.html (last accessed: 1/12/2020).

Bloom, Allan, *The Closing of the American Mind* (New York: Simon and Schuster, 1987).

Booth, Wayne, *The Company We Keep: An Ethics of Fiction* (Berkeley: University of California Press, 1988).

Borschel-Dan, Amanda, 'From "Heil Hitler" to "Shalom, Tel Aviv," the Many Incarnations of David Bowie' *The Times of Israel* 11/1/2016 www.timesofisrael.com/from-heil-hitler-to-shalom-tel-aviv-the-many-incarnations-of-david-bowie/ (last accessed: 1/12/2020).

Bowie, David, 'Manuscript Notes on 1. Outside' (1995), Courtesy of the David Bowie Archive, exhibited at the Victoria and Albert Museum in 2013. See Johnson, 2015, 1–18.

Bowie, David, 'Live in Berlin' 22/9/2002 www.youtube.com/watch?v=a8NBpfkpyZw (last accessed: 1/12/2020).

Boyd, William, *Nat Tate: An American Artist 1928–1960 (1998)* (London: Penguin, 2020).

Boyd, William, 'William Boyd: How David Bowie and I Hoaxed the Art World' *The Guardian* 12/1/2016 www.theguardian.com/music/2016/jan/12/art-david-bowie-william-boyd-nat-tate-editor-critic-modern-painters-publisher (last accessed: 1/12/2020).

Brackett, David (ed), *The Pop, Rock and Soul Reader* (Oxford: Oxford University Press, 2005).

Brackmann, Rebecca, 'Dwarves Are Not Heroes: Antisemitism and the Dwarves in J.R.R. Tolkien's Writing' (2010) 28(3) *Mythlore* https://dc.swosu.edu/cgi/viewcontent.cgi?article=1172&context=mythlore (last accessed: 1/12/2020).

Braga, Matthew, 'The Verbasizer Was David Bowie's 1995 Lyric Writing Mac App' *Vice* 11/1/2016 www.vice.com/en_us/article/xygxpn/the-verbasizer-was-david-bowies-1995-lyric-writing-mac-app (last accessed: 1/12/2020).

Braidotti, Rosi, 'Teratologies' in Claire Colebrook and Ian Buchanan (eds) *Deleuze and Feminism* (Edinburgh: Edinburgh University Press, 2000) pp. 156–179.

Braidotti, Rosi, *The Posthuman* (Boston: Polity Press, 2013).

Brooker, Will, *Forever Stardust: David Bowie Across the Universe* (London: I.B. Tauris, 2017).

Brooker, Will, *Why Bowie Matters* (London: William Collins, 2019).

Brown, Mick, 'Interview of David Bowie: "I Have Done Just About Everything That It's Possible to Do"' *The Telegraph* 14/12/1999 (republished in *The Telegraph* 10/1/2017) www.telegraph.co.uk/music/artists/david-bowie-interview-from-1996-i-have-done-just-about-everythin/ (last accessed: 1/12/2020).

Browning, Gordon Frederick, *Tristan Tzara: The Genesis of the Dada Poem, of from Dada to Aa* (Stuggart: Akademischer Verlag Heinz, 1979).

Bruckner, Pascal, *Perpetual Euphoria: On the Duty to be Happy* (Princeton, NJ: Princeton University Press, 2011).

Buckley, David, *Strange Fascination: Bowie: The Definitive Story* (London: Virgin Books, 2005).

Buñuel, Luis, 'Preface to the Script for Un Chien Andalou' (1929) *La Revolution Surrealiste* (no. 12) 12/12/1929.

Buñuel, Luis, *My Last Sigh* (London: Vintage, 1984).

Burke, Edmund, *A Philosophical Enquiry into the Origin of Our Ideas of the Sublime and Beautiful (1757)* (London: Penguin, 1998).

Burroughs, William S., *Minutes to Go* (Paris: Two Cities Edition, 1960).

Burroughs, William S., *Naked Lunch (1959)* (New York: Grove Press, 1964).

Burroughs, William S., *The Wild Boys: A Book of the Dead* (New York: Grove Press, 1971).

Burroughs, Williams S., *Queer* (London: Penguin, 1985).

Burroughs, William S., *The Job: Interviews with William Burroughs* (New York: Penguin, 1989).

Burroughs, William S, *The Adding Machine (1985)* (New York: Grove Press, 2013).

Butler, Judith, *Gender Trouble: Feminism and the Subversion of Identity* (New York: Routledge, 1990).

Butler, Judith, *Bodies That Matter: On the Discursive Limits of Sex* (New York: Routledge, 1993).

Butler, Judith, *Undoing Gender* (London: Routledge, 2004).

Canguilhem, Georges, 'Monstrosity and the Monstrous' (1964) 40 *Diogenes* 27–42.

Cann, Kevin, *Any Day Now – David Bowie: The London Years: 1947–1974* (Croyden, Surrey: Adelita, 2010).

Carr, Roy and Shaar Murray, Charles, *Bowie: An Illustrated Record* (New York: Avon, 1981).

Carroll, Noel, *The Philosophy of Horror: Paradoxes of the Heart* (London: Routledge, 1990).

Carroll, Noel, 'Moderate Moralism' (1996) 36 *British Journal of Aesthetics* 223–238.

Carson, Anne, 'Decreation: How Women Like Sappho, Marguerite Porete and Simone Weil Tell God' in *Decreation* (New York: Knopf, 2005) pp. 155–183.

Cavanagh, David, 'Changes Fifty Bowie' Q *Magazine* 2/1997, pp. 52–59.

Caveney, Graham, *The 'Priest' They Called Him: The Life and Legacy of William S. Burroughs* (London: Bloomsbury, 1998).

Cavna, Michael, 'Beyond the Music: How David Bowie Was One of Our Smartest Visual Artists' *The Washington Post* 11/1/2016 www.washingtonpost.com/news/comic-riffs/wp/2016/01/11/beyond-the-music-how-david-bowie-was-one-of-our-smartest-visual-artists-as-well/ (last accessed: 1/12/2020).

Chaplin, Charles, *The Great Dictator* (Los Angeles, CA: United Artists, 1940).

Cinque, Toija, Moore, Christopher and Redmond, Sean (eds) *Enchanting David Bowie: Space, Time, Body, Memory* (London: Bloomsbury, 2015).

Cinque, Toija and Redmond, Sean, *The Fandom of David Bowie: Everyone Says 'Hi'* (London: Palgrave Macmillan, 2019).

Cockburn, Harry, 'France Considers Banning Gitanes and Gauloises Cigarettes for Being "Too Cool"' *The Independent* 21/7/2016 www.independent.co.uk/news/world/europe/france-banning-gitanes-and-gauloises-cigarettes-too-cool-a7148701.html (last accessed: 1/12/2020).

Cohen, Jeffrey J., 'Monster Culture: Seven Theses' in Jeffrey J. Cohen (ed) *Monster Theory: Reading Culture* (Minneapolis: University of Minnesota Press, 1996).

Cohen, Jeffrey J., *Of Giants: Sex, Monsters and the Middle Ages* (Minneapolis: University of Minnesota Press, 1999).

Coke, Edward, *The Institutes of the Laws of England 1628–1644* vol 1–4 (New York: Garland Publishing, 1979).

Cooper, Anneliese, 'David Bowie's Sincerity' in Theodore G. Ammon (ed) *David Bowie and Philosophy: Rebel Rebel* (Chicago: Open Court, 2016) pp. 139–148.

Copetas, Craig, 'Beat Godfather Meets Glitter Mainman: William Burroughs Interviews David Bowie,' *Rolling Stone* 28/2/1974 www.rollingstone.com/music/music-news/beat-godfather-meets-glitter-mainman-william-burroughs-interviews-david-bowie-92508/) (last accessed: 1/12/2020).

Cordner, Christopher, 'F. R. Leavis and the Moral in Literature' in Richard Freadman and Lloyd Reinhardt (eds) *On Literary Theory and Philosophy* (London: Palgrave Macmillan, 1991).

Cray, Ed, *Ramblin' Man: The Life and Times of Woody Guthrie* (New York: Norton, 2006).

Crenshaw, Kimberlé et al (eds), *Critical Race Theory: The Key Writings That Formed the Movement* (New York: The New Press, 1996).

Critchley, Simon, *The Faith of the Faithless* (New York: Verso, 2012).

Critchley, Simon, *Infinitely Demanding* (New York: Verso, 2013).

Critchley, Simon, *Bowie* (New York: OR Books, 2014).

Critchley, Simon, *On Bowie* (London: Serpents Tail, 2016).

Crowe, Cameron, 'David Bowie: Ground Control to Davy Jones' *Rolling Stone Magazine* 12/2/1976 www.rollingstone.com/music/music-news/david-bowie-ground-control-to-davy-jones-77059/ (1976a) (last accessed: 1/12/2020).

Crowe, Cameron, 'A Candid Conversation with the Actor, Rock Singer and Sexual Switch-Hitter' *Playboy Magazine* 9/1976b www.playboy.com/read/playboy-interview-david-bowie (last accessed: 1/12/2020).

Crowley, Aleister, *White Stains (1898)* (Scotts Valley, CA: CreateSpace Independent Publishing Platform, 2008).

Crowley, Aleister, *The Book of the Law (1904)* (Scotts Valley, CA: CreateSpace Independent Publishing Platform, 2018).

Curcio, James (ed), *Masks: Bowie & Artists of Artifice* (Chicago, IL: Intellect, 2020).

D'Adamo, Amedeo, 'Is Bowie Our Kirkegaard? A Theory of Agency in Fandom' (2019) 10 *Celebrity Studies* 60–74.

Daily Mirror, 'Bowie Rules the Pool, OK!' *Daily Mirror* 4 May 1976.

Danto, Arthur, *Nietzsche as Philosopher* (New York: Columbia University Press, 1965).

D'Arms, Justin and Jacobson, Daniel, 'The Moralistic Fallacy: On the "Appropriateness" of Emotions' (2000) 61 *Philosophy and Phenomenological Research* 65–90.

Daston, Lorraine, 'Marvelous Facts and Miraculous Evidence in Early Modern Europe' (1991) 18 *Critical Inquiry* 93–124.

Davidson, Arnold, 'The Horror of Monsters' in James J. Sheehan and Morton Sosna (eds) *The Boundaries of Humanity: Humans, Animals, Machines* (Berkeley: California University Press, 1991) pp. 36–67.

Davies, Stephen, 'Beardsley and the Autonomy of the Work of Art' (2005) 63 *Journal of Aesthetics and Art Criticism* 179–183.

de Beauvoir, Simone, *The Second Sex (1949)* (London: Vintage, 1997).

de Bracton, Henry, *On the Laws and Customs of England 1240–1260* vol 1–4 (Cambridge: Harvard University Press, 1968).

DeCurtis, Anthony, 'I'm Not Quite an Atheist, and It Worries Me' Interview with David Bowie, *Beliefnet* 6/2003 www.beliefnet.com/entertainment/2005/07/im-not-quite-an-atheist-and-it-worries-me.aspx (last accessed: 1/12/2020).

Debord, Guy, *Society of the Spectacle* (London: Rebel Press, 1994).

Delgado, Richard and Stefancic, Jean (eds), *The Latino/a Condition: A Critical Reader* (New York: New York University Press, 1998).

Derrida, Jacques, 'Passages – From Traumatism to Promise' in E. Weber (ed) *Points . . . Interviews, 1974–1994* (Stanford: Stanford University Press, 1995) pp. 372–395.

Derrida, Jacques, *Writing and Difference (1967)* (London: Routledge, 2001).

Derrida, Jacques, *The Politics of Friendship* (London: Verso, 2005).

Devereaux, Mary, 'Beauty and Evil: The Case of Leni Riefenstahl's Triumph of the Will' in Jerrold Levinson (ed) *Aesthetics and Ethics: Essays at the Intersection* (Cambridge: Cambridge University Press, 1998) pp. 227–256.

Devereux, Eoin, Dillane, Aileen and Power, Martin J. (eds), *David Bowie: Critical Perspectives* (London: Routledge, 2015).

Doggett, Peter, *The Man Who Sold the World: David Bowie in the* 1970s (London: The Bodley Head, 2011).

Dollimore, Jonathan, 'Different Desires: Subjectivity and Transgression in Wilde and Gide' (1987) 1(1) *Textual Practice* 48–67.

Drury, Nevill, 'The Thelemic Sex Magick of Aleister Crowley' in Nevill Drury (ed) *Pathways in Modern Western Magic* (Richmond, CA: Concrescent Scholars, 2012).

Durkheim, Émile, 'On the Normality of Crime (1895)' in Talcott Parsons et al (eds) *Theories of Society: Foundations of Modern Sociological Theory* (New York: Free Press of Glencoe, 1965a) pp. 872–875.

Durkheim, Émile, *The Elementary Forms of Religious Life (1912)* (New York: The Free Press, 1965b).

Eaton, Anne M., 'Robust Immoralism' (2012) 70(3) *Journal of Aesthetics & Art Criticism* 281–292.

Eliot, T. S., 'The Function of Criticism' (1923) 2(5) *Criterion* 38.

Eliot, T. S., *The Waste Land and Other Poems* (London: Faber and Faber, 2002).

Ellis, Katie et al (eds), *Manifestos for the Future of Critical Disability Studies* vol 1 (New York: Routledge, 2018).

Elsaesser, Thomas, 'From Mastering the Past to Managing Guilt' in *German Cinema, Terror and Trauma: Cultural Memory Since 1945* (New York: Routledge, 2014) pp. 263–305.

Emerson, Ken, 'Rolling Stone' 8/1974 www.rollingstone.com/music/music-album-reviews/diamond-dogs-112951/ (last accessed: 1/12/2020).

Eno, Brian, *Oblique Strategies: Over One Hundred Worthwhile Dilemmas* (London: Brian Eno, 1979).

Eno, Brian on Twitter @dark_shark 6/3/2017.

Epstein, Julia, *Altered Conditions: Disease, Medicine, and Storytelling* (London: Routledge, 1995).

Erlich, Nancy, 'Bowie, Bolan, Heron – Superstars?' *The New York Times* 11/7/1971 www.nytimes.com/1971/07/11/archives/bowie-bolan-heron-superstars.html (last accessed: 1/12/2020).

Fanning, Dave, 'Interview with David Bowie, RTE Irish Radio' 1997 www.youtube.com/watch?v=_3SfX6h5ouM (last accessed: 1/12/2020).

Fanon, Frantz, *Black Skin, White Masks (1952)* (London: Penguin, 2020).

Ferreira, Daniel, 'Verbasizer (David Bowie)' *7luas* 30/10/2013 www.7luas.com.br/all/research/researchblog/verbasizer-david-bowie-eng/ (last accessed: 1/12/2020).

Fitch, Richard, 'In This Age of Grand Allusion: Bowie, Nihilism and Meaning' in Eoin Devereux, Aileen Dillane and Martin J. Power (eds) *David Bowie: Critical Perspectives* (London: Routledge, 2015) pp. 19–34.

Fleming, Colin, 'Remembering Bod Dylan's Infamous "Judas" Show' *Rolling Stone* 17/5/2016 www.rollingstone.com/music/music-news/remembering-bob-dylans-infamous-judas-show-203760/ (last accessed: 1/12/2020).

Fornäs, Johan, 'The Future of Rock: Discourses That Struggle to Define a Genre' (1995) 14(1) *Popular Music* 111–125.

Fossett, Katelyn, 'David Bowie's Strange Politics' *Politico Magazine* 13/1/2016 www.polit ico.com/magazine/story/2016/01/david-bowie-death-politics-213529/ (last accessed: 1/12/2020).

Foucault, Michel, *The Archaeology of Knowledge* (New York: Pantheon, 1972).

Foucault, Michel, *Discipline and Punish: The Birth of the Prison* (London: Penguin, 1977).

Foucault, Michel, *Herculine Barbin: Being the Recently Discovered Memoirs of a Nineteenth Century French Hermaphrodite* (New York: Pantheon Books, 1980a).

Foucault, Michel, *The History of Sexuality vol 1: An Introduction* (New York: Vintage, 1980b).

Foucault, Michel, 'Preface to the English Edition' in Gilles Deleuze and Felix Guattari (eds) *Anti-Oedipus: Capitalism and Schizophrenia.* Translated from the French by Robert Hurley, Mark Seem and Helen R. Lane (Minneapolis: University of Minnesota, 1983).

Foucault, Michel, *Michel Foucault: Politics, Philosophy and Culture – Interviews and Other Writings, 1977–1984* (ed) Lawrence D. Kritzman (New York: Routledge, 1988a).

Foucault, Michel, 'An Aesthetics of Existence' in Lawrence D. Kritzman (ed) *Michel Foucault: Politics, Philosophy, Culture – Interviews and Other Writings, 1977–1984* (New York: Routledge, 1988b) pp. 47–53.

Foucault, Michel, *Ethics: Subjectivity and Truth vol 1 Essential Works of Foucault 1954–1984* (ed) Paul Rabinow (London: Penguin, 1997).

Foucault, Michel, *Abnormal: Lectures at the College of France 1974–75* (London: Verso, 2003).

Fox, Dan, *Pretentiousness: Why It Matters* (Minneapolis, MN: Coffee House Press, 2016).

Fraser, Michael, 'The Compassion of Zarathustra: Nietzsche on Sympathy and Strength' (2006) 68(1) *The Review of Politics* 49–78.

Freud, Sigmund, *The Uncanny (1919)* (New York: Penguin, 2003).

Frith, Simon, *Sound Effects: Youth, Leisure, and the Politics of Rock 'n' Roll* (New York: Pantheon, 1981).

Fromm, Eric, *The Fear of Freedom (1942)* (London: Routledge, 2001).

Fudge, Erica, *Perceiving Animals: Humans and Beasts in Early Modern English Culture* (London: Palgrave Macmillan, 2000).

Fuss, Diana (ed), *Inside/Out: Lesbian Theories, Gay Theories* (New York: Routledge, 1991).

Gane, Nicholas, 'Posthuman' (2005) 23(2–3) *Theory, Culture & Society* 431–434.

Gaut, Berys, *Art, Emotion and Ethics* (Oxford: Oxford University Press, 2007).

Geck, Martin, *Richard Wagner: A Life in Music* (trans) Stewart Spencer (Chicago: Chicago University Press, 2013).

Gill, Andy, 'David Bowie: How the Outsider's Outsider Proved Himself Far Braver Than the Rock 'n' Roll Mainstream' *The Independent* 11/1/2016 www.independent.co.uk/arts-entertainment/music/features/david-bowie-how-the-outsiders-outsider-proved-him self-far-braver-than-the-rock-n-roll-mainstream-a6806791.html (last accessed: 1/12/2020).

Girard, Rene, *The Scapegoat* (Baltimore, MD: Johns Hopkins University Press, 1986).

Gontarski, Stanley E., 'Weaponised Aesthetics and Dystopian Modernism: Cut-Ups, Playbacks, Pick-Ups and the "Limits of Control" from Burroughs to Deleuze' (2020) 14(4) *Deleuze and Guattari Studies* 555–584.

Goodall, Howard, 'Bowie: Music, Lucky Old Sun is in My Sky. . .' in Geoffrey Marsh and Victoria Broackes (eds) *David Bowie Is* (London: V&A Publishing, 2013).

Goodman, Jessica, 'Rolling Stones: David Bowie "Was an Extraordinary Artist"' *Entertainment* 11/1/2016 https://ew.com/article/2016/01/11/rolling-stones-remember-david-bowie/ (last accessed: 1/12/2020).

Graham, Elaine L., *Representations of the Post-Human: Monsters, Aliens and Others in Popular Culture* (New Brunswick, NJ: Rutgers University Press, 2002).

Gregory, Jason, 'Rolling Stones Guitarist Keith Richards Slams David Bowie' *Gigwise* 30/4/2008 www.gigwise.com/news/42820/ (last accessed: 1/12/2020).

Grossberg, Lawrence, 'The Media Economy of Rock Culture: Cinema, Post-Modernity and Authenticity' in Simon Firth, Andrew Goodwin and Lawrence Grossberg (eds) *Sound and Vision: The Music Video Reader* (London: Routledge, 1993).

Gutman, Robert, *Richard Wagner: The Man, His Mind and His Music (1968)* (San Diego, CA: Harcourt Brace Jovanovich, 1990).

Gysin, Brion and Burroughs, William S., *The Exterminator* (San Francisco: Auerhahn, 1960).

Gysin, Brion and Burroughs, William S., *The Third Mind* (New York: Viking, 1978).

Hanafi, Zakiya, *The Monster in the Machine: Magic, Medicine and the Marvelous in the Time of the Scientific Revolution* (Durham, NC: Duke University Press, 2000).

Haraway, Donna, 'Manifesto for Cyborgs: Science, Technology, and Socialist Feminism' (1985) 86 *Socialist Review* 65–107.

Harford, Tim, *Messy: The Power of Disorder to Transform Our Lives* (New York: Riverhead Books, 2016).

Harris, Oliver, 'Can You See a Virus? The Queer Cold War of William Burroughs' (1999) 33(2) *Journal of American Studies* 243–266.

Harris, Oliver, 'Introduction' in *William S. Burroughs Nova Express: The Cut-Up Trilogy: The Restored Texts* (ed) Oliver Harris (New York: Penguin, 2014).

Hassan, Ihab, 'The Subtracting Machine: The Work of William Burroughs' (1963) 6(1) *Critique: Studies in Modern Fiction* 4–23.

Hebdige, Dick, *Subculture: The Meaning of Style* (London: Routledge, 1995).

Hegel, Georg W.F., *The Phenomenology of Mind (1807)* vol 2 (London: Routledge, 2002).

Heidegger, Martin, *Being and Time (1927)* (London: Wiley-Blackwell, 1978).

Herbermann, Charles G., *The Catholic Encyclopedia* vol 7 (Charleston, SC: Nabu Press, 2010).

Hesketh, Roger, *Fortitude: The D-Day Deception Campaign* (New York: Overlook Press, 2002).

Het Popgebeuren, Dutch Chat Show, 'Interview with David Bowie in Hotel de L'Europe Amsterdam' 14/101977 www.youtube.com/watch?v=VudyGkGWDlc (last accessed: 1/12/2020).

Hilburn, Robert, 'Bowie Finds His Voice' *Melody Maker* 14 September 1974.

Hill, Kevin, 'David Bowie, Political Philosopher?' in Theodore G. Ammon (ed) *David Bowie and Philosophy: Rebel Rebel* (Chicago: Open Court, 2016) pp. 71–83.

Holm-Hudson, Kevin, 'Who Can I Be Now? David Bowie's Vocal Persona' (2018) 37(3) *Contemporary Music Review* 214–234.

hooks, bell, *Ain't I a Woman: Black Women and Feminism* (Boston: South End Press, 1981).

Humphries, Patrick, *Nick Drake: The Biography* (London: Bloomsbury, 1998).

Hunt, Kevin J., 'The Eyes of David Bowie' in Toija Cinque, Christopher Moore and Sean Redmond (eds) *Enchanting David Bowie: Space, Time, Body, Memory* (London: Bloomsbury, 2015).

Idel, Moshe, *Kabbalah: New Perspectives* (New Haven, CT: Yale University Press, 1988).

Irigaray, Luce, *This Sex Which Is Not One* (Ithaca, NY: Cornell University Press, 1985).

Jacobson, Daniel, 'In Praise of Immoral Art' (1997) 25 *Philosophical Topics* 155–199.

Jancovich, Mark, *The Cultural Politics of the New Criticism* (Cambridge: Cambridge University Press, 1993).

Johnson, Alex, 'The Book List: David Bowie's Top 100 Reads – from Lady Chatterley's Lover to 1984,' *The Independent* 13/3/2018 www.independent.co.uk/arts-entertainment/

books/features/david-bowie-influencers-books-literature-book-list-orwell-music-crea tive-a8252801.html (last accessed: 1/12/2020).

Johnson, Kathryn, 'David Bowie Is' in Eoin Devereux, Aileen Dillane and Martin J. Power (eds) *David Bowie: Critical Perspectives* (London: Routledge, 2015) pp. 1–18.

Jones, Allan, 'Goodbye to Ziggy and All That' *Melody Maker* October 1977.

Jones, Dylan, *When Ziggy Played Guitar: David Bowie and Four Minutes That Shook the World* (London: Random House, 2012).

Jones, Dylan, *David Bowie: A Life* (London: Windmill Books, 2018).

Joyce, James, *Finegan's Wake* (London: Penguin, 2000).

Julius, Anthony, *Transgressions: The Offences of Art* (London: Thames and Hudson, 2002).

Kafer, Alison, *Feminist, Queer, Crip* (Bloomington, IN: Indiana University Press, 2013).

Kant, Immanuel, *Critique of Judgment (1790)* (Oxford: Oxford University Press, 2009).

Karchilaki, Maria, 'Interview with David Bowie' 2002 www.youtube.com/ watch?v=ohb3IAWt4cs&t=549s (last accessed: 1/12/2020).

Keightley, Kier, 'Reconsidering Rock' in Simon Frith, Will Straw and John Street (eds) *The Cambridge Companion to Rock and Pop* (Cambridge: Cambridge University Press, 2001) pp. 109–142.

Ketcham, Chris, 'David Bowie's Sadness' in Theodore G. Ammon (ed) *David Bowie and Philosophy: Rebel Rebel* (Chicago: Open Court, 2016) pp. 173–186.

Kieran, Matthew, 'Forbidden Knowledge: The Challenge of Immoralism' in José Luis Ber-múdez and Sebastian Gardner (eds) *Art and Morality* (London: Routledge, 2003).

Kimmelman, Michael, 'David Bowie on His Favorite Artists,' Interview with David Bowie, *New York Times* 14/1/1998.

Kirkegaard, Soren, *Works of Love (1847)* (New York: Harper Perennial, 2009).

Kivy, Peter, *Authenticities: Philosophical Reflections on Musical Performance* (Ithaca, NY: Cornell University Press, 1995).

Kohn, Sally, 'David Bowie's Mind-Blowing Queer Legacy,' *Refinery* 11 January 2016.

Kristeva, Julia, *Powers of Horror: An Essay on Abjection (1980)* (New York: Columbia University Press, 1984).

Kumari-Campbell, Fiona, *Contours of Ableism: The Production of Disability and Abledness* (London: Palgrave Macmillan, 2009).

Lampert, Matthew, 'The Madness of the Musician' in Theodore G. Ammon (ed) *David Bowie and Philosophy: Rebel Rebel* (Chicago: Open Court, 2016) pp. 151–172.

Land, Christopher, 'Apomorphine Silence: Cutting-Up Burroughs' Theory of Language and Control' (2005) 5(3) *Ephemera: Theory & Politics in Organization* 450–471.

Landry, Donna (ed), *The Spivak Reader: Selected Works of Gayatri Chakravorty Spivak* (London: Routledge, 1996).

Lasch, Christopher, *The Culture of Narcissism: American Life in an Age of Diminishing Expecta-tions* (New York: Norton, 1979).

Laqueur, Thomas, *Making Sex: Body and Gender from the Greeks to Freud* (Cambridge, MA: Harvard University Press, 1990).

Leigh, Wendy, *Bowie: The Biography* (New York: Gallery Books, 2014).

Levinas, Emmanuel, 'Ethics and Spirit' in S. Hand (trans) *Difficult Freedom: Essays on Judaism (1963)* (Baltimore, MD: Johns Hopkins University Press, 1997).

Levinas, Emmanuel, *Totality and Infinity (1961)* (Pittsburgh, PA: Duquesne University Press, 1999).

Light, Alan, 'How David Bowie Brought Thin White Duke to Life on Station to Sta-tion' *Rolling Stone* 23/1/2017 www.rollingstone.com/music/music-features/how-david-bowie-brought-thin-white-duke-to-life-on-station-to-station-125797/ (last accessed: 1/12/2020).

Lindberg, Ulf, Guomundsson, Gestur, Michaelsen, Morten and Weisethaunet, Hans, *Rock Criticism from the Beginning: Amusers, Bruisers, and Cool-Headed Cruisers* (New York: Peter Lang, 2005).

Lindholm, Charles, *Culture and Authenticity* (Malden: Blackwell, 2008).

Lindsay, Matthew, 'The Hideous Ecstasy of Fear: Diamond Dogs 40 Years on' *The Quietus* 11/1/2016 https://thequietus.com/articles/16797-the-hideous-ecstasy-of-fear-diamond-dogs-40-years-on (last accessed: 1/12/2020).

Littmann, Greg, 'Squawking Like a Pink Monkey Bird – What?' in Theodore G. Ammon (ed) *David Bowie and Philosophy: Rebel Rebel* (Chicago: Open Court, 2016) pp. 47–58.

Lovejoy, Arthur O., *The Great Chain of Being: A Study of the History of an Idea* (Cambridge, MA: Harvard University Press, 1970).

Lykke, Nina and Braidotti, Rosi (eds), *Between Monsters, Goddesses and Cyborgs: Feminist Confrontations with Science, Medicine and Cyberspace* (London: Zed Books, 1996).

MacDonald, Ian, 'David Bowie: The Revolution Is Here' *New Musical Express* 17/3/1973 www.rocksbackpages.com/Library/Article/david-bowie-the-revolution-is-here (last accessed: 1/12/2020).

MacDonald, Ian, 'David Bowie: White Lines, Black Magic' *Uncut* 10/1998 www.rocksbackpages.com/Library/Article/david-bowie-white-lines-black-magic (last accessed: 1/12/2020).

MacDonald, Ian, 'John Martyn: "Bowie's a Poseur" – A Classic Interview from the Vaults' *The Guardian* 11/9/2013 www.theguardian.com/music/2013/sep/11/john-martyn-from-rocks-backpages (last accessed: 1/12/2020).

MacKinnon, Angus, 'The Future Isn't What It Used to Be,' *New Music Express* 13/9/1980 www.bowiegoldenyears.com/articles/800913-nme.html (last accessed: 1/12/2020).

MacKinnon, Catherine, *Feminism Unmodified: Discourses of Life and Law* (Cambridge, MA: Harvard University Press, 1988).

Manderson, Desmond, 'Leftovers: The End of Private Law' (2006) 29 *Vendredi* 23–144.

Mazillo, Mark, 'The Man Who the World Sold: Kurt Cobain, Rock's Progressive Aesthetic, and the Challenge of Authenticity' (2000) 84(4) *The Musical Quarterly* 713–749.

McLeod, Ken, 'Space Oddities: Aliens, Futurism and Meaning in Popular Music' (2003) 22(3) *Popular Music* 337–355.

McLuhan, Marshall, *Understanding Media* (London: Routledge, 1964).

McMahon, James, 'The Shooting of John Lennon: Will Mark Chapman Ever Be Released?' *The Independent* 10/12/2020 www.independent.co.uk/arts-entertainment/music/features/john-lennon-shooting-murder-anniversary-death-mark-david-chapman-jail-yoko-ono-b1767795.html (last accessed: 10/12/2020).

McRuer, Robert, *Crip Theory: Cultural Signs of Queerness and Disability* (New York: New York University Press, 2006).

Metzger, Gustav, *Damaged Nature, Auto Destructive Art* (London: Coracle Press, 1999).

Middleton, Richard, 'Articulating Musical Meaning/Re-constructing Musical History/Locating the "Popular"' in Richard Middleton and David Horn (eds) *Popular Music* vol 5 (Cambridge: Cambridge University Press, 1985).

Miles, Barry, *Bowie in His Own Words* (London: Omnibus Press, 1984).

Millner, Jacqueline, Moore, Catriona and Cole, Georgina, 'Art and Feminism: Twenty-First Century Perspectives' (2015) 15(2) *Australian and New Zealand Journal of Art* 143–149.

Moore, Allan, 'Authenticity as Authentication' (2002) 21(2) *Popular Music* 209–223.

Morgan Britton, Luke, 'Charlie Watts Says David Bowie Wasn't a "Musical Genius" and It "Wouldn't Bother" Him If Rolling Stones Split' *New Musical Express* 27/2/2018 www.nme.com/news/music/charlie-watts-david-bowie-rolling-stones-split-2249606 (last accessed: 1/12/2020).

Morley, Paul, 'Siouxsie Sioux: "I've Always felt on the Outside" – A Classic Interview from the Vaults' *The Guardian* 16/10/2012 www.theguardian.com/music/2012/oct/16/siouxsie-banshees-classic-interview (last accessed: 1/12/2020).

Morley, Paul, *The Age of Bowie: How David Bowie Made a World of Difference* (London: Simon & Schuster, 2016).

Mottram, Eric, *William Burroughs: The Algebra of Need* (London: Marion Boyars, 1977).

MTV, 'Interview with David Bowie' 1995 www.youtube.com/watch?v=zri74q3HDDY (last accessed: 1/12/2020).

Muchall, Martin, 'Bowie the Buddhist' in Theodore G. Ammon (ed) *David Bowie and Philosophy: Rebel Rebel* (Chicago: Open Court, 2016) pp. 59–70.

Murphy, Peter, 'Review: Ever the Absolute Beginner: *Bowie* by Simon Critchley' *The Irish Times* 18/10/2014 www.irishtimes.com/culture/books/ever-the-absolute-beginner-bowie-by-simon-critchley-1.1965934 (last accessed: 1/12/2020).

Musician's Union, 'The MU's Response to David Bowie's "Nazi Salute"' 1976 www.muhistory.com/from-the-archive-2-mu-response-to-david-bowies-nazi-salute/ (last accessed: 1/12/2020).

Nabokov, Vladimir, *Lolita* (London: Penguin, 2000).

Nehamas, Alexander, *Nietzsche: Life as Literature* (Cambridge, MA: Harvard University Press, 1985).

Nicholas, Barry and Metzger, Ernest, *An Introduction to Roman Law* (Oxford: Oxford University Press, 1976).

Nietzsche, Friedrich, *The Will to Power* (trans) Walter Kaufmann and Reginald John Hollingdale (1883–1888 Notebooks) (New York: Vintage Books, 1968).

Nietzsche, Friedrich, *Thus Spoke Zarathustra (1885)* (London: Penguin, 1974).

Nietzsche, Friedrich, 'Twilight of the Idols' in Walter Kaufmann (ed) *The Portable Nietzsche (1889)* (New York: Penguin, 1976a) pp. 463–563.

Nietzsche, Friedrich, 'The Antichrist' in Walter Kaufmann (ed) *The Portable Nietzsche (1895)* (New York: Penguin, 1976b) pp. 569–656.

Nietzsche, Friedrich, *The Birth of Tragedy from the Spirit of Music (1872)* (London: Penguin, 1993).

Nietzsche, Friedrich, *Human, All Too Human: A Book for Free Spirits (1878)* (New York: Penguin, 1994).

Nietzsche, Friedrich, *Beyond Good and Evil (1886)* (London: Penguin, 2003).

Nietzsche, Friedrich, *The Gay Science (1882)* (Cambridge: Cambridge University Press, 2019).

Nussbaum, Martha, 'Pity and Mercy: Nietzsche's Stoicism' in Richard Schacht (ed) *Nietzsche, Genealogy, Morality: Essays on Nietzsche's on the Genealogy of Morals* (Berkeley, CA: University of California Press, 1994) pp. 139–167.

O'Grady, Anthony, 'David Bowie: "Rock and Roll Is Dead"' *RAM* 26/7/1975a www.rocksbackpages.com/Library/Article/david-bowie-rock-and-roll-is-dead (last accessed: 1/12/2020).

O'Grady, Anthony, 'David Bowie: Watch Out Mate! Hitler's on His Way Back' *NME* 8/1975b https://thequietus.com/articles/03598-david-bowie-nme-interview-about-adolf-hitler-and-new-nazi-rock-movement (last accessed: 1/12/2020).

O'Leary, Chris, 'Pushing Ahead of the Dame: David Bowie, Song by Song "Sweet Thing"' 23/9/2010a https://bowiesongs.wordpress.com/2010/09/23/sweet-thing-candidate-sweet-thing-reprise/ (last accessed: 1/12/2020).

O'Leary, Chris, 'Pushing Ahead of the Dame: David Bowie, Song by Song "Station to Station"' 23/12/2010b https://bowiesongs.wordpress.com/2010/12/23/station-to-station/ (last accessed: 1/12/2020).

O'Leary, Chris, 'Pushing Ahead of the Dame: David Bowie, Song by Song "Heathen"' 10/6/2014 https://bowiesongs.wordpress.com/?s=Heathen (last accessed: 1/12/2020).

Oppenheim, Maya, 'David Bowie: How the Glam Rock Artist Became an LGBT Icon' *The Independent* 11/1/2016 www.independent.co.uk/news/people/how-david-bowie-became-a-gay-icon-a6806041.html (last accessed: 1/12/2020).

Orwell, George, *1984 (1949)* (London: Penguin, 2004).

Orwell, George, 'Benefit of Clergy: Some Notes on Salvador Dali' in *All Art Is Propaganda: Critical Essays* (New York: Mariner Books, 2008) pp. 210–222.

Outka, Gene, *Agape: An Ethical Analysis* (New Haven, CT: Yale University Press, 1977).

Paré, Ambroise, *On Monsters and Marvels* (Chicago: University of Chicago Press, 1982).

Parret, Herman, 'Kant on Music and the Hierarchy of the Arts' (1998) 56(3) *Journal of Aesthetics and Art Criticism* 251–264.

Paxman, Jeremy, 'Interview with David Bowie' *BBC* 1999 www.youtube.com/watch?v=LaHcOs7mhfU (last accessed: 1/12/2020).

Pearce, Joseph, 'Nazism & Narcissism: David Bowie's Flirtation with Fascism' *The Imaginative Conservative* 19/2/2016 https://theimaginativeconservative.org/2016/02/nazism-and-narcissism-david-bowie-flirtation-with-fascism.html (last accessed: 1/12/2020).

Pegg, Nicholas, *The Complete David Bowie* (London: Reynolds & Hearn, 2002).

Peraino, Judith A., 'Plumbing the Surface of Sound and Vision: David Bowie, Andy Warhol and the Art of Posing' (2012) 21(1) *Qui Parle* 151–179.

Peters, Michael A., 'The Fascism in Our Heads: Reich, Fromm, Foucault, Deleuze and Guattari – the Pathology of Fascism in the 21st Century' (2020) *Educational Philosophy and Theory* www.tandfonline.com/doi/full/10.1080/00131857.2020.1727403 (last accessed: 1/12/2020).

Phillips, David, *Exhibiting Authenticity* (Manchester: Manchester University Press, 1997).

Potter, Michael K. and Cobb, Cam, 'David Bowie and Death' in Theodore G. Ammon (ed) *David Bowie and Philosophy: Rebel Rebel* (Chicago: Open Court, 2016) pp. 111–125.

Potter, Terry, 'When David Bowie and Eric Clapton Flirted with the Far-Right and Inspired an Anti-Fascist Movement' *Public Reading Rooms: The Politics of Art and Vice Versa* 4/8/2016 https://prruk.org/when-david-bowie-and-eric-clapton-flirted-with-the-far-right-and-inspired-an-anti-fascist-movement/ (last accessed: 1/12/2020).

Pratt, Ray, 'The Politics of Authenticity in Popular Music: The Case of the Blues' (1986) 10(3) *Popular Music and Society* 55–78.

Prosser, Jay, *Second Skins: The Body Narratives of Transsexuality* (New York: Columbia University Press, 1998).

Rae, Casey, *William S. Burroughs and the Cult of Rock 'n' Roll* (Austin, TX: University of Texas Press, 2019).

Razinsky, Hili, *Ambivalence: A Philosophical Exploration* (New York: Rowman & Littlefield, 2016).

Redmond, Sean, 'Who Am I Now? Remembering the Enchanted Dogs of David Bowie' (2013) 4(3) *Celebrity Studies* 380–383.

Regardie, Israel, *The Tree of Life* (Portland, OR: LLewellyn Publications, 2001).

Regardie, Israel, *The Complete Golden Dawn System of Magic* (Scottsdale, AZ: New Falcon Publications, 2015).

Reisch, George, 'The Actor Tells the Truth' in Theodore G. Ammon (ed) *David Bowie and Philosophy: Rebel Rebel* (Chicago: Open Court, 2016) pp. 3–8.

Rich, Adrienne, 'Compulsory Heterosexuality and Lesbian Existence' (1980) 5 *Signs: Journal of Women in Culture and Society* 631–660.

Richardson, *Nietzsche's System* (Oxford: Oxford University Press, 1996).

Robert, Jason S. and Baylis, Francoise, 'Crossing Species Boundaries' (2003) 3 *American Journal of Bioethics* 1–13.

Roberts, Chris, 'Action Painting' *Ikon* 10/1995 www.rocksbackpages.com/Library/Article/david-bowie-action-painting (last accessed: 1/12/2020).

Roberts, Chris, '"I'm Hungry for Reality" *Uncut Magazine* 10/1999 www.uncut.co.uk/features/david-bowie-i-m-hungry-for-reality-part-4-27210/ (last accessed: 1/12/2020).

Rock, Mick, *Blood and Glitter* (London: Vision on Publishing, 2001).

Rook, Jean, 'Waiting for Bowie, and Finding a Genius Who Insists He's Really a Clown', *Daily Express* 5 May 1976.

Rorabaugh, W.J., *American Hippies* (New York: Cambridge University Press, 2015).

Rossinow, Douglas, *The Politics of Authenticity: Liberalism, Christianity and the New Left in America* (New York: Columbia University Press, 1998).

Rousseau, Jean-Jacques, *The Confessions* (London: Penguin, 1973).

Rowland, Beryl, *Animals with Human Faces: A Guide to Animal Symbolism* (London: Allen & Unwin, 1974).

Rubridge, Sarah, 'Does Authenticity Matter? The Case for and Against Authenticity in the Performing Arts' in Patrick Campbell (ed) *Analysing Performance* (Manchester: Manchester University Press, 1996) pp. 219–233.

Said, Edward, *Orientalism (1978)* (London: Penguin, 2003).

Saint Clair, Ericson, 'Comunicacao E Rock and Roll: O Perspectivismo Por David Bowie' (2002) 2(2) *Contemporanea* 202.

Saint Matthew, *King James Bible* (Oxford: Oxford University Press, 2008).

Saint Paul, 'Letter to Ephesians' in *King James Bible* (Oxford: Oxford University Press, 2008).

Salinger, J.D., *Catcher in the Rye (1951)* (London: Penguin, 2010).

Salisbury, Joyce E., *The Beast Within: Animals in the Middle Ages* (London: Routledge, 1994).

Sartre, Jean-Paul, *Being and Nothingness (1943)* (London: Routledge, 2018).

Sauchelli, Andrea, 'Ethicism and Immoral Cognitivism: Gaut Versus Kieran on Art and Morality' (2012) 46(3) *The Journal of Aesthetic Education* 107–118.

Savage, Jon, 'David Bowie: Gender Bender' *The Face* 11/1980 www.rocksbackpages.com/Library/Article/david-bowie-the-gender-bender (last accessed: 1/12/2020).

Savage, Jon, *England's Dreaming: The Sex Pistols and Punk Rock* (London: Faber and Faber, 2005).

Schacht, Richard, *Nietzsche* (London: Routledge, 1983).

Scheler, Max, 'Agape as Superabundant Vitality: A Response to Nietzsche' in David L. Norton and Mary F. Kille (ed) *Philosophies of Love* (New York: Chandler Publishing Company, 1971) pp. 191–199.

Schellekens, Elisabeth, 'Evaluating Art Morally' *Theoria* 2020 https://onlinelibrary.wiley.com/doi/full/10.1111/theo.12294 (last accessed: 15/1/2021).

Schopenhauer, Arthur, *The World as Will and Representation (1844)* vol 2 (New York: Dover Publications, 2000).

Schopenhauer, Arthur, *On the Suffering of the World (1850)* (London: Penguin, 2004).

Sedgwick, Eve, *The Epistemology of the Closet* (London: Penguin, 1990).

Serano, Julia, *Whipping Girl: A Transsexual Woman on Sexism and the Scapegoating of Femininity* (Emeryville, CA: Seal Press, 2007).

Shaar Murray, Charles, 'Goodbye Ziggy and a Big Hello to Aladdin Sane' *New Musical Express* 27/1/1973.

Shaar Murray, Charles, '244 Words on Punk from David Bowie' *New Musical Express* 29/10/1977.

Shakespeare, William, *The Tempest: The Oxford Shakespeare* (Oxford: Oxford University Press, 2008).

Sharpe, Alex, *Foucault's Monsters and the Challenge of Law* (London: Routledge, 2010).

Sharpe, Alex, 'Scary Monsters: The Hopeful Undecidability of David Bowie 1947–2016' (2017) 11(2) *Law and Humanities* 228–244.

Sheffield, Rob, *On Bowie* (London: Headline, 2016).

Shelley, Mary, *Frankenstein: Or, the Modern Prometheus (1818)* (London: Collins, 2010).

Shildrick, Margrit, *Embodying the Monster: Encounters with the Vulnerable Self* (London: Sage, 2002).

Shuker, Roy, *Popular Music Culture: The Key Concepts* (London: Routledge, 2012).

Spelman, Elizabeth, *Inessential Woman: Problems of Exclusion in Feminist Thought* (New York: Beacon Press, 1988).

Spitz, Marc, *Bowie: A Biography* (London: Aurum Press, 2009).

Stark, Tanja, ' "Crashing Out with Sylvian": David Bowie, Carl Jung and the Unconscious' in E. Devereux, A. Dillane and M.J. Power (eds) *David Bowie: Critical Perspectives* (New York: Routledge, 2015a).

Stark, Tanja, 'Confronting Bowie's Mysterious Corpses' in Christopher Moore and Sean Redmond (eds) *Enchanting David Bowie: Space Time Body Memory* (London: Bloomsbury, 2015b) pp. 61–77.

Stevenson, Robert Louis, *The Strange Case of Dr Jekyll and Mr Hyde* (Munich: Deutscher Taschenbuch Verlag, 1986).

Stewart, Tony, 'Heil and Farewell,' *New Musical Express* 8/5/1976 www.rocksbackpages. com/Library/Article/david-bowie-heil-and-farewell (last accessed: 1/12/2020).

Stryker, Susan and Whittle, Stephen, *The Transgender Studies Reader* (London: Routledge, 2006).

Sturzaker, Doreen and Sturzaker, James, *Colour and the Kabbalah* (York Beach, ME: Samuel Weiser, Inc, 1975).

Stychin, Carl F., *Law's Desire: Sexuality and the Limits of Justice* (London: Routledge, 1995).

Tan, Monica, 'How David Bowie Turned Down Coldplay: "It's not a Very Good Song, Is It?" ' 20/1/2016 www.theguardian.com/music/2016/jan/20/how-david-bowie-turned-down-coldplay-its-not-a-very-good-song-is-it (last accessed: 1/12/2020).

Taylor, Charles, *Sources of the Self: The Making of the Modern Identity* (Cambridge: Cambridge University Press, 1989).

Taylor, Charles, *The Ethics of Authenticity* (Cambridge: Harvard University Press, 1991).

Thomas, Keith, *Man and the Natural World: A History of Modern Sensibility* (London: Lane, 1983).

Tolstoy, Leo, *What Is Art?* (trans) A. Maude (Oxford: Oxford University Press, 1930).

Trilling, Lionel, *Sincerity and Authenticity* (Cambridge: Harvard University Press, 1972).

Trynka, Paul, *Starman: David Bowie: The Definitive Biography* (London: Sphere, 2011).

Usher, Bethany and Fremaux, Stephanie, 'Turn Myself to Face Me: David Bowie in the 1990s and Discovery of Authentic Self' in Eoin Devereux, Aileen Dillane and Martin J. Power (eds) *David Bowie: Critical Perspectives* (London: Routledge, 2015) pp. 56–81.

Vanity Fair, 'David Bowie Answers the Proust Questionnaire' 11/1/2016 (originally published in 8/1998) www.vanityfair.com/hollywood/2016/01/david-bowie-proust-questionnaire (last accessed: 1/12/2020).

Von Appen, Ralph and Doehring, Andre, 'Nevermind the Beatles, Here's Exile 61 and Nico: "The Top 100 Records of All Time" – a Canon of Pop and Rock Albums from a Sociological and an Aesthetic Perspective' (2006) 25 *Popular Music* 21–39.

Waldrep, Shelton, *Future Nostalgia: Performing David Bowie* (London: Bloomsbury, 2015).

Wale, Michael, 'David Bowie: Festival Hall' *The Times* 7/1972.

Warner, Michael, *Fear of a Queer Planet: Queer Politics and Social Theory* (Minneapolis, MN: University of Minnesota Press, 1993).

Watts, Michael, 'Oh You Pretty Things,' Interview with David Bowie, *Melody Maker* 22/1/1972 www.rocksbackpages.com/Library/Article/oh-you-pretty-thing-david-bowie- (last accessed: 1/12/2020).

Weinstein, Deena, 'Art Versus Commerce: Deconstructing a (Useful) Romantic Illusion' in Karen Kelly and Evelyn McDonnell (eds) *Stars Don't Stand Still in the Sky: Music and Myth* (London: Routledge, 1999) pp. 57–69.

Weisethaunet, Hans and Lindberg, Ulf, 'Authenticity Revisited: The Rock Critic and the Changing Real' (2010) 33(4) *Popular Music and Society* 465–485.

White, Timothy, 'Turn and Face the Strange' *Crawdaddy* 2/1978 www.bowiegoldenyears. com/press/78-02-00-crawdaddy.html (last accessed: 1/12/2020).

Wilcken, Hugo, *Low* (New York: Continuum, 2005).

Wilde, Oscar, *The Picture of Dorian Gray (1890)* (London: Penguin, 2003).

Williams, Patricia, *The Alchemy of Race and Rights* (Cambridge, MA: Harvard University Press, 1992).

Yentob, Alan, 'Cracked Actor Documentary' 1975 www.youtube.com/watch?v=PmVR FEfjiwM (last accessed: 1/12/2020).

Young, Iris Marion, *Justice and the Politics of Difference* (Princeton, NJ: Princeton University Press, 1990).

Žižek, Slavoj, *Everything You Always Wanted to Know About Lacan but Were Afraid to Ask Hitchcock* (London: Verso, 2010).

INDEX

'1984' (song) 64

abnormal individuals 15, 18–19, 21n22
Acker, Kathy 59
Aesop's fable of the Golden Goose 53n43
aestheticism 42; *see also* autonomism
aesthetic properties 51
'aesthetic relevance' 42, 44–45, 49, 51, 53n43
aesthetics 5–6, 22n40
aesthetic value 5, 6, 41–44, 49
affective-cognitive states 44; *see also* cognitive-affective responses
affective relationships with fans/listeners 7, 65, 74
'After All' (song) 67n7
agape 1, 7, 73–74, 79, 81
AIDS/HIV 22n63
'Alabama Song' (Brecht & Weill) 55n76
Aladdin Sane xi, 4, 8n38, 19, 32, 37n86
Aladdin Sane (album) 19, 22n52, 55n93, 62, 81n3
alienation 8n19, 28
aliens: Burroughs on non-viral 61; imagery of androgynous 18; in *The Man Who Fell to Earth* 4, 17, 33; as a messiah 32, 37n86, 45, 54n53; as metaphor for God 77; Thomas Jerome Newton 33, 79; *see also* Ziggy Stardust
'All the Young Dudes' (song) 31, 36n62
allusion 3, 22n52, 32, 36n82
Alomar, Carlos 54n69, 66, 69n71
ambiguity 17, 18–20, 22n46, 49, 65

ambivalence 5, 44, 49
'An Occasional Dream' (song) 68n33
androgynous individuals 18, 19, 33, 59
androids 21n13; *see also* robots
'Andy Warhol' (song) 36n46
animality 80
antihero 44
anti-semitism 41, 52n4, 54n61, 56n106
Anttonen, Veikko 21n29
aristocrats 18, 46
Armistead, Claire 68n38
art/artwork: *agape* as a theme in Bowie's 81; ambivalence in 49; attitude of Bowie's 46, 49–51, 55–56n106; authenticity in 29; auto-destructive 76, 82n36; autonomism and 6; censorship of 41; cognitive engagement with 42; conceptual 36n78; as confession 29; derivative nature of 34; of Duchamp 36n78; estrangement from 51; ethical defects in 49, 51; ethical limits of 1, 3; ethical properties of 45, 49, 51, 53n43; ethics and 1, 5–6, 41–45, 53n15; evaluating 5, 41, 51, 52n11; fascism and 1, 41; harm from 41; 'homoerotic' 52n1; immoralism and 43–45; moralism and 42, 45, 53n15; morality and 41, 43–45, 49, 51; Nat Tate art world hoax 27, 35n13; and offence 41; opacity in immoralist 43; paintings 42, 76; pedagogic/moral case for 44; philosophy of 42; power and 5; "pure 'signature' in the Warholian sense" 35n22; realist 80;

sense of immediacy in xiv, 31; and the sublime 43; as testimony 29; Thin White Duke and 5–6, 41–42; transgressive 4, 5, 17, 41, 49; as unstable 32; *see also* music
artifice 19, 27–28, 30–34, 35n22; *see also* inauthenticity
artists: 'artistic self' of 29; authenticity of 1, 29–34; character of 56n106; cut-ups and creative blockage of 6, 60, 61, 66; intention of 49, 55–56n106
atheist 78
attachment 76
Attali, Jacques 3
attraction–repulsion dynamic 77
Augustine (Saint) 16
authenticity 1–2, 4–5, 27–34, 35n25, 66; *see also* inauthenticity
autobiographical lyrics 6, 63
auto-destructive art 76, 82n36
autonomism 6, 42–43
avant-garde 2, 32

Baal xii, 8n35
Baal (play) 4, 8n35, 17
Bach, Johann Sebastian 2–3, 50
Badiou, Alain 7, 74, 76, 79, 81n2
Bangs, Lester 27, 49
Barbin, Herculine 16
Bart, Lionel 18, 22n42
Barthes, Roland 32
Bauman, Zygmunt 4, 21n6
Beardsley, Monroe 53n17
'Beauty and the Beast' (song) 17, 21n35
Beethoven, Ludwig van 2–3, 50
Benjamin, Walter 45
Berlin years (1977–1979): electronic music and 51, 69n74; Eno collaboration during 51, 56n120, 69n72, 69n74; Kraftwerk's, Can and Neu's influence on 22n43, 48, 50, 69n74; relationship with Ronny Haag during 19; *see also Heroes* (album); *Lodger* (album); *Low* (album); Thin White Duke
Bertolucci, Bernardo 46
bestial humans 14
bestiality 80
'Big Brother' (song) 64
bisexuality 19–20, 81n5
Blackstar (album) 20, 79, 81n3, 83n77
Blackstone, William 21n2
Blaylock, John 79
blues music 29
Bogart, Humphrey 59
Bono 78
Bowie, Angie 19

Bowie, David: on acting 33; on aesthetics 22n40; on artifice 28; on being "authentic" 28; Burroughs and xiii, 31, 35n22, 59–60, 63; cocaine and 47, 54n69; creation of 32, 36n84; criticism of 27, 35n6; on cut-ups 6, 61–63, 67n24; death of 3, 20; on desire to be more than human 17, 79; on dreams 62; Eliot and 62, 68n38; emotions in music of 33–34; eyes of 17; as fan of other artists 8n24; fascism, interest in 1, 47, 51–52, 56n106; on finding 'the real me' 30; on "future nostalgia" 20; on gender performances of rock stars 47; Haag and 19; on Hitler 46; on integrity 28; Kemp and 37n96; and the Lower Third (band) 62, 67n28; on the mainstream 18; on messages in his work 30; on being a Messiah 54n53; narrative in early lyrics of 62; Nazis, fascination with 45–47, 54n48; on originality 36n71, 36n74; on Pierrot 52; on postmodernism 28; as postmodern rock star 3, 28, 35n22; on power of rock stars 47; on "presumptuousness of the songwriter" 31; on pretensions 28; on relationship with fans 45–50, 75; religion and 77, 83n64; on rock 'n' roll 68n52; *Rolling Stone* interview with, by Burroughs 36n54, 60, 62, 68n38; as 'second wave' composer 2–3; sexuality of 19–20, 81n5; and spirituality of 77, 78; studio albums by 22n39; as thief 6, 60, 67n9; on Thin White Duke 46–47; totalitarianism, interest in 45, 47; on *The Wild Boys* 69n63; *see also* Jones, David
Bowie knife 60, 67n8, 69n63
Bowie love 7, 73–81, 84n101
Boyd, William 35n13
Bracton, Henry de 13, 21n2
Bradiotti, Rosi 79
'Breaking Glass' (song) 54n47
Brecht, Bertolt 4, 8n35, 17, 48, 55n76
Brel, Jacques 3, 81n3
bricoleur 60
Brooker, Will 2, 32
Bruckner, Anton 50
Buckley, David 8n38, 48
Buddha of Suburbia (album) 78, 83n61
Buddhism, Tibetan 77
Buñuel, Luis 48
Burgess, Anthony 37n93
Burke, Edmund 9n55

Burroughs, William S: as 'beat godfather'
59; Bowie and xiii, 31, 35n22, 59–60,
63; on Bowie knife 67n8; culture,
interest in contemporary 59–60; death,
interest in 59; Eliot and 61, 67n26;
on the future 67n24; heroin-induced
paranoia of 61, 67n16; influence of
67n3; Joyce and 61; on killing of
wife 67n5; on language 6, 61, 67n16;
madness, interest in 59; *Naked Lunch*
65; on non-viral aliens 61; *Nova Express*
60, 61, 63; occult, interest in 59; *Rolling
Stone* interview by, with Bowie 36n54,
60, 62, 68n38; science fiction, interest
in 59, 67n24; sex, interest in 59; space,
interest in 59; as thief 67n9; on time
travel 67n6; *The Wild Boys* 65, 67n8,
69n63; *see also* cut-ups writing method,
Burroughs'
'Bus Stop' (song) 78, 83n63
Butler, Judith 81

cabaret 19
Cabaret (play/film) 48
cacophonous music 32
cacophony 33, 64
Can (band) 69n74
Canguilhem, Georges 4, 13–16, 21n4,
21n19
'Can't Help Thinking About Me' (song)
62, 67n28
capitalism 28, 75
Carroll, Noel 19
Carson, Anne 81
Catcher in the Rye (Salinger) 35n11
Cauldfield, Holden 27, 35n11
Cavani, Liliana 46
censorship 41, 52n5
chameleon 18
change 17, 18, 76–77, 82n44
'Chant of the Ever Circling Skeletal Family'
(song) 64
Chaplin, Charlie 56n126
Chapman, Mark 27, 35n11
Christianity: *agape* 1, 7, 73–74, 79, 81;
Bowie and 77–78; cross in 48, 55n97;
crusades and 77–78; Holy Grail,
Himmler's quest for 54n48, 68n33;
humility in 77; love of God in 73; 'The
Next Day' (song) on priesthood 78;
Nietzsche on 73; self-effacing love in
84n101
Churchill, Winston 45
Cinque, Toija 2, 8n19

cis-sexuality 19, 22n64
classical music 50
Classical Period 14
Clockwork Orange (film) 33, 37n93
"closet heterosexual" 19, 22n63
cocaine 47, 54n69, 56n116, 65, 69n68
Cock Rock music 19, 22n55
cognitive-affective responses 44, 45, 51
cognitive self-mastery 79
Cohen, Jeffrey 4, 5, 16
Coke, Edward 21n2
Coldplay (band) 78, 83n71
collective dreams 31
collective unconscious 62
community 5, 34, 35n29, 76
compassion 74, 82nn15–16
complexity 17, 44
complicity 44, 51
Coney Island Cavalcade Variety Show
83n88
confession 29, 34
Conformist, The (film) 46
conjoined twins 14
connection 17, 20
consciousness 61
continental philosophy 4
control 60, 61, 67n16
Cookie Monster 14–15
Cooper, Anneliese 65
Covid-19 pandemic xiv
creativity: boredom as enemy of 66; Bowie
and 8n24, 63, 74; community and 5, 34;
compassion and 74; cut-ups and 6, 60;
joy in xii; narcissism and xi; Nietzsche
on 74
Critchley, Simon: on affirmation of life 80;
on authenticity 2, 5, 28–29; on *Diamond
Dogs* album 63–64; fan perspective of
2; Heidegger and 68n50; on illusion 32;
on inauthenticity 30, 32; on Lazarus 20;
on love 2, 81; on mood and voice 63;
on Nietzsche 83n68; on religion and
Bowie 78, 83n68; on self reinvention
4; on Thin White Duke's Stockholm
interview 54n61; on transcendence 78;
on yearning 75
critical disability studies 4
critical race theory 4, 43
cross, Christian 48, 55n97
Crowe, Cameron 54n53, 55n70
Crowley, Aleister 53–54n47, 56n113,
67n7, 77
crusades 77–78
Cubism 36n78

culture: Bowie's artwork challenging
notions of 51; Burroughs' and Bowie's
interest in contemporary 59–60;
Diamond Dogs album as study of 63;
hippie 31; inner life and 31; norms of
28–29; popular 2, 3, 17; refusal to 'sell
out' in rock 29; taboo in Western 80
Curcio, James 31–32, 50
cut-ups writing method, Burroughs':
affective experience through 63;
authenticity and 34, 66; Bowie on 6,
63, 67n24; creativity and 6, 60; *Diamond
Dogs* album and 6, 60, 63–66; digitalised
version of 63; discussion on 6, 59–66;
felt reality and 6, 61; identity and 61;
images in 6, 62–63, 65, 66; the ineffable
conveyed through 6, 63; in language war
6, 61; listener's creative agency and 6,
64; politico-theoretical significance of
60–61; premonitions of the future and
67n24; purposes of 6, 60–61; random
outcomes and 60–61; temporality altered
by 67n24; transformation of Bowie's
writing using 60
cyborgs 21n13, 83n80; *see also* robots
'Cygnet Committee' (song) 31

Dada 36n78
Dadaism 59
D'Adamo, Amedeo 76
Daily Mirror (newspaper) 55n87
Dali, Salvador 48, 53n22
David Bowie (album) 54n53, 68n33, 77,
82n48
death: of Bowie 3, 20; Bowie's lyrics on
81n3; Burroughs' and Bowie's interest
in 59; of personas 76, 82n38; stasis
equals, in art/artwork 18, 59; Western
philosophers' preoccupation with 73
decadence 47, 48
defamiliarisation 43
deformed/disabled 21n5
degenerates 4, 17
Deleuze, Giles 67n16
de minimis principle 42
demystification process 75–76
derivation 31, 32
Derrida, Jacques 4, 14, 16
desire: to affirm life 74; Bowie's, to be more
than human 17, 79; to censor art/artwork
52n5; Foucault on 47; for freedom 47;
monster as amalgam of fear and 17; to
plan accidents 66; for power 49, 51;
repressed 48; sexual 19; for spirit 78

detournement 31, 36n56
Devereaux, Eoin; Dillane, Aileen; and
Power, Martin J. 2
devil 50, 78, 80, 83n87
Diamond Dogs (album): '1984' on 64;
ambiguity and dissonance and 65; 'Big
Brother' on 64; 'Chant of the Ever
Circling Skeletal Family' on 64; cover
of 80, 83n84, 83nn87–88; Critchley
on 63–64; cut-ups and 6, 60, 63–66;
'Diamond Dogs' on 64, 68n59; Doggett
on 63; as dystopian 5, 64; Emerson
on 68n55; 'Future Legend' on 64, 65;
Halloween Jack persona and 4, 32;
leader/follower relationship and 50;
opacity and 64–65; operatic approach
to music on 22n60; Orwell's *1984* and
5, 45, 64; post-apocalyptic soundscape
on 63–64; punk music and 64–65;
soul music and 64; the sublime 64;
'Sweet Thing/Candidate/Sweet Thing
(Reprise)' on 33, 63–65, 69n68; themes
in 65; totalitarianism in 45; as transitional
album 64; 'We are the Dead' on 64
'Diamond Dogs' (song) 64, 68n59
Dickens, Johanna 83n88
dictatorship 46
Dietrich, Marlene 19
difference: between animals and humans
80; artistic authenticity and 1; Badiou
on 7, 74; Butler on 81; in continental
philosophy 4; in critical disability studies
4; in critical race theory 4; in feminism
4; between humans and monsters 13,
15; vs. identity 7, 74, 76; love and 79;
manifestation of 75; in postcolonial
theory 4; posthumanism and 79; in
queer theory 4; social norms not valuing
7, 75; in trans theory 4
Dionysus xii
disco music 51
discordant music 18, 33, 65
dissonance, lyrical and musical 32, 65
divine 21n28, 53n47; *see also* God; gods
Doggett, Peter 48, 51, 63, 65
Drake, Nick 27
dreams 31, 50, 62, 63
'Drive-in Saturday' (song) 62
Droogs 37n93
Duchamp, Marcel 32, 36n78
Du Noyer, Paul 51
Durkheim, Émile 21n28, 43
Dylan, Bob 30, 77
dystopia/dystopian 5, 16, 32, 45, 64

Earthling (album) 78, 83n69
Eaton, Anne 44, 53n16
Edward VIII (King) 46
Egyptian Sphinx photo shoot 80,
    83n83
'Eight Line Poem' (song) 62, 68n38
electronic music 51, 69n74, 79
Elephant Man, The (play) 4, 8n37, 17,
    27, 79
Eliot, T. S. 43, 61, 62, 67n26, 68n38
Emerson, Ken 68n55
emotional authenticity 33–34
Cinque, Toija et al 2
Eno, Brian 51, 56n120, 65–66, 69n70,
    69n72, 69n74
Ephesians, Letter to (Saint Paul) 50
estrangement 43, 44, 51; *see also*
    transgression
ethical attitude 44–45, 49
ethical defects 42–45, 49, 51
ethical freedom 81
ethical limits 1, 3
ethical merits 42–45
ethical properties 42, 45, 49, 51, 53n43
ethical value 6, 41, 49
ethicism 52n13
ethics: art/artwork and 1, 5–6, 41–45,
    53n15; Bowie as a figure of xi; fascism
    and 1, 41; Foucault on 81; immoralism
    and 43–45; moralism and 42, 45, 53n15;
    of Nietzsche 82n15; otherness and 7, 73,
    79; philosophy of art and 42; power and
    5; 'of self-deification' 74; Thin White
    Duke and 5–6, 41–42
'European canon' 50
exorcism 50, 56n116
expressionism 27, 33, 35n13, 48

fake 28
fakers 20; *see also* personas
fakery 19, 33
'Fame' (song) 47, 55n80
fans: as active agents 34; affective
    relationships with 7, 65; as creative
    community 5, 34; ethical relations
    with 78; interpretations of lyrics by 32,
    36n77; leader/follower relationship and
    5, 45–50; love and mourning of 76–77
'Fantastic Voyage' (song) 67n27
fascism: art, ethics, and 1, 41; attitude
    of Bowie's artwork towards 49–51;
    Bowie's interest in 1, 47, 51–52, 56n106;
    caricatured 51; endorsement of 50;
    Foucault on 47; imagery, allure of 46;

and love of power 47; "resurgence of
    interest in" 46; Thin White Duke flirting
    with 5, 33, 41, 45–50, 54n61; *Un Chien
    Andalou* and 48; *see also* Nazis
feminism 4, 43
fidelity 18, 67n7
fiery darts 50
fisson 19–20
Fitch, Richard 36n82, 75
'Five Years' (song) 77
folk music 18, 29–30, 36n52, 77
Foucault, Michel: on abnormal individuals
    15, 21n22; on "becoming" 30; on bestial
    humans 14; and Burroughs' ideas on
    language as a virus 67n16; on concern
    for the other 84n101; on conjoined
    twins 14; on desire 47; on ethics 81; on
    fascism 47; on freedom 75, 81, 84n101;
    on hermaphrodites 14, 16, 18; on law
    15; on monsters 4, 13–16, 21n4, 21n22;
    on monstrosity and monstrousness 19,
    21n19; on the "possibility of being
    otherwise" 7, 75; on psyche 15;
    on self, care for 84n101; on 'soul' 15;
    on 'truth' 30
fragmentation 31, 33
Fraser, Michael 82n15
freak 4
freedom: to become 7; desire for 47; ethical
    81; Foucault on 75, 81, 84n101; love
    and 7, 75–76; social norms and 75; of
    spirit 78; as supreme principle of life
    21n29; totalitarianism as "flight
    from" 47
Free Trade Hall 77
Fromm, Eric 47
funk 18, 51, 64, 68n54
fusion 19–20
future: Bowie on the 75; Burroughs on
    the 67n24; community 76; Derrida on
    the 16; dystopian 5, 45; hopeful, vs.
    repetitive tomorrows 4; monsters and the
    16–17
'Future Legend' (song) 64, 65
"future nostalgia" 20
futurism 48
futuristic music 48

Galen of Pergamum 22n46
"Garbo" (Juan Pujol Garcia) 45, 54n51
Garbo, Greta 19
Garcia, Juan Pujol 45, 54n51
Garland, Judy 33
Garson, Mike 64, 68n56

Gaut, Berys 42, 44, 49, 52n13, 53n43, 56n106
gay 19–20, 52n1, 81n5; *see also* homosexuality
Gay Science (Nietzsche) 83n68
gender: ambiguity about 18–20; authenticity and ideas of 30; constructedness of 19; cultural insignia of 19; *Diamond Dogs* album and 65; fans' relationships with Bowie and narratives of 8n19; of monsters 18; performances of rock stars 47; transgender 81n5; *see also* androgynous individuals
gender identity 22n64
Genet, Jean 19, 22n52
genitalia 80
genius 18, 22n41, 28, 35n22, 63
Genome Project 80
genre 18, 32, 34, 51, 67n7, 67n24
German expressionism 33
German fascism 47
German modernism 32
Gide, Andre 19
Girard, Rene 4, 21n6
Gitanes cigarettes 48, 55n90
glam rock music 64
Gnosticism 77
God: aliens as a metaphor for 77; art and music as dialogue with 74; Bowie's search for 63; 'Bus Stop' (song) on 78; conflict between devil and 50; in "Great Chain of Being" 84n92; *Heathen* album and 78; humility in recognition of the self in relation to 77; love of 73; Nietzsche on 83n68; Saint Augustine on monsters as signs from 16
'God' (song) 31, 36n64
gods: Apollo 47; Baal xii, 8n35; Bowie on musicians as 79, 83n68; Dionysus xii; law from 20; vs. monsters 14, 20; Bowie canonised or deified as 14; 'tragic endless lives' of 20; in a world without, place of the sacred in 4, 16, 17
Godzilla 14–15
Goebbels, Paul Joseph 54n48
'Golden Years' (song) 19, 50, 51
Goodall, Howard 2
"Great Chain of Being" world view 80, 84n92
Great Dictator, The (film) 56n126
Greco-Christian idea of a love for humanity (*agape*) 1, 7, 73–74, 79, 81
the Griffin 21n4

grunge music 29
Guthrie, Woody 30, 36n52
Gysin, Brion 59

Haag, Romy 19
Halloween Jack 4, 32
Hanafi, Zakiya 13
Haraway, Donna 79, 80, 83n80
Harris, Oliver 59, 67n3
Hayes, Issac 64, 68n54
Haze, Dolores 52n2
Heathen (album) 23n73, 69n71, 77–79, 83nn54–55
'Heathen' (song) 23n73, 78–79
heathen, idea of man-God as 74
Heckel, Erich 3
Hegel, Georg Wilhelm Friedrich 28
Heidegger, Martin 35n25, 68n50
hermaphrodites 14, 16, 18
Hermetic Qabalah 45, 48, 53n47, 56n116, 77, 82n52
Heroes (album): Alomar's work on 69n71; 'Beauty and the Beast' (song) on 17, 21n35; Eno collaboration on 56n120, 69n74; slogan used to advertise 3, 8n18
heterosexuality 19, 20, 22n63
Hill, Kevin 47
Himmler, Heinrich 54n48, 68n33
hip hop music 29
hippies 18, 31, 32
Hitchcock, Alfred 1
Hitler, Adolf 45–48, 50, 54n51; *see also* Nazis
HIV/AIDS crisis 22n63
'Hollow Men, The' (poem) 68n38
Holm-Hudson, Kevin 79
Holocaust 56n106
Holy Grail, Himmler's quest for 54n48, 68n33
'homoerotic art' 52n1
homophobia 19
homo sapiens 80; *see also* humans
homosexuality 19, 22n52; *see also* gay
hopefulness 4, 14, 16–17
hubris 77
human/animal 14, 18, 21n10, 79–80, 83n80, 83nn87–88
humanism 79
humans: boundaries of 83n80; Burroughs' on language's parasitic relationship with 6, 61, 67n16; "destruction and rearticulation of" 20; difference between monsters and 13, 15; 'genetic essence' of 84n94; Genome Project 80; in "Great

Chain of Being" 84n92; posthuman 7, 79–81
Humbert Humbert 53n16
humility 7, 44, 77–79
Hunger, The (film) 4, 8n36, 17
Hunky Dory (album): 'Andy Warhol' on 36n46; cover of 19, 83n83; 'Eight Line Poem' on 62, 68n38; Nietzsche and 81n7; 'Oh, You Pretty Things' on 73, 81n9; 'Quicksand' on 45, 53–54n47, 68n33, 77, 81n3
hybridity: Bowie offering 20; embracing 80–81; human/animal 14, 18, 21n10, 79–80, 83n80, 83nn87–88; vs. Nazi racial purity 51; vs. ontological purity 80; posthumanism and 79–80

'I Can't Give Everything Away' (song) 79, 83n77
identity: authenticity and 31; Badiou on 7, 74; cut-ups and 61; vs. difference 7, 74, 76; gender 22n64; of hermaphrodites 16; language and 6, 61; posthumanism and 79; sexual 19; tyranny of fixed 18
ideological cluster 13
ideology 7, 45, 51, 75; *see also* social norms
idiot 21n5
illusion 32–34
image and stardom 27
imagery 18, 45–46, 52n1
images: in cut-ups 6, 62–63, 65, 66; on *Diamond Dogs* cover 80, 83n84, 83nn87–88; from Egyptian Sphinx photo shoot 83n83; on *Hunky Dory* cover 19, 83n83; of Jesus Christ 52n3; on *The Man Who Sold the World* cover 19; of Nazis 45; of Nuremberg rallies 5; on *Station to Station* back cover 54n47; in 'Sweet Thing/Candidate/Sweet Thing (Reprise)' 33; in *Un Chien Andalou* 48
imagination 31, 64
imaginative resistance 44
imitation 31
immediacy xiv, 30, 31, 36n54, 63
immoral attitude 45
immoralism 6, 43–45, 49, 51, 82n15
immoral literature 53n17
imperfectability 79
impermanence 76
impurity 20
inauthenticity: Bowie accused of 5, 27–28; Critchley on 30, 32; truth of iii, 1, 5, 32, 34; *see also* artifice; authenticity
Incredible Hulk (Marvel Comics) 14, 19

indifference 44
individualism 31
ineffable 6, 63, 66
infidelity 32, 34
inner life 29–30, 31, 35n29
intersex individuals 18; *see also* hermaphrodites
Isolar world tour (1976) 41, 43, 50–51, 54n47, 55n80
Isolar world tour (1978) 9n53, 52n9
isopsephy, ancient Greek 53n47
'I would be Your Slave' (song) 77, 83n55

Jacobson, Daniel 43
Jagger, Mick 46, 59, 67n9
'Janine' (song) 31, 36n68
Japanese Kabuki theatre costumes 33, 76
jazz music 29
'Jean Genie' (song) 19, 22n52
Jekyll and Hyde 14, 19
Jesus Christ 23n77, 48, 52n3, 73–74; *see also* Christianity
Jews/Judaism 53n47, 56n106, 77
John Lennon/Plastic Ono Band (album) 36n64
Jones, David 30, 36n84; *see also* Bowie, David
Jones, Davy 36n84
Joyce, James 61
Julius, Anthony 43
Jung, Carl 62, 68n35
Justinian's Code 13, 20n1

Kabbalah 53n47, 77
Kabuki theatre 33, 76
Kant, Immanuel 9n55, 43, 68n43
'Karma Man' (song) 77
Keats, John 35n26
Kemp, Lindsay 33, 37n96
Kether 53n47, 77
Kieran, Matthew 43–44
'Kingdom Comes' (song) 81n3
King Kong 14–15
Kirkegaard, Soren 81n2
Kivy, Peter 28
Kraftwerk (band) 22n43, 48, 50, 69n74
Krautrock 18, 33
Kubrick, Stanley 33, 37n93

Lacan, Jacques 1
Land, Christopher 61
language: Burroughs on 6, 61, 67n16; distrust of language on *Low* album 66;

Foucault on 67n16; indeterminacy of 3; monsters and 17; Schopenhauer on music as universal 68n43; self-perception and 66; *see also* narratives
Laqueur, Thomas 22n46
Lasch, Charles 31
Last Temptation of Christ, The (film) 55n97
law: breach of, monster as a 4, 15, 21n4; Canguilhem on 15; of the Christian church 78; a crisis of classification in 15; Crowley on 67n7; English common, on monsters 13, 21n2; Foucault on 15; from the gods 20; love and 1, 74; monsters who laugh at 1
'Law (Earthlings on Fire)' (song) 78, 83n69
'Lazarus' (song) 20, 81n3
Lazarus, resurrection of 23n77
Leavis, F. R. 42, 53n15
Legendary Stardust Cowboy 33, 37n94
Lennon, John 20, 27, 31, 36n64
leper 21n5
'Let Me Sleep Beside You' (song) 62
'Letter to Hermione' (song) 62
Levinas, Emmanuel 73, 81n2
Lewis, Alzoria 83n88
liberalism 28, 46
life: affirmation of 74, 78, 80; *Heathen* album addressing 78; inner 29–30, 31, 35n29; Nietzsche on 73–74; *see also* Tree of Life
Lindholm, Charles 35n25
Lindsay, Matthew 64
Lindsay Kemp troupe 37n96
linguistic control 60
Lodger (album) 18, 56n120, 67n27, 69n71, 69n72, 69n74
Lolita (Nabokov) 41, 52n2
love: *agape* 1, 7, 73–74, 79, 81; as antithetical to law 1; Badiou on 74; Bowie love 7, 73–81, 84n101; Carson on self and 81; change and 76–77; Christianity's love of God 73; Critchley on 2, 81; difference and 79; an ethic of 76; freedom and 7, 75–76; as humility 7, 77–79; as letting go 7, 76–77; longing for 20; monsters and 17; Nietzsche's 'tough love' 74; philosophers on 73, 81n2; as posthuman 7, 79–81; of power 47, 50; self reinvention and 4; social norms and 75; yearning for 75
'Loving the Alien' (song) 77–78
Low (album): Alomar's work on 69n71; 'Breaking Glass' on 54n47; distrust of language on 66; Eno collaboration on 56n120, 69n74; side two instrumentals on 43, 66; 'Subterraneans' on 66, 69n77; 'Warszawa' on 66, 69n75
lunatic 21n5
Lutheran, Bowie as iconoclastic 78
lyrics: allusion in 32, 36n82; autobiographical 6, 63; cut-up 6, 34, 60, 63–66; on death 81n3; and discordant music 65; dream references in 62; Eno's *Oblique Strategies* for writing 65; interpretations of, by fans 32, 36n77; linear narrative structure and 65

madness 31–32, 46, 59
Mahler, Gustav 50
Malkuth 53n47, 77
Manderson, Desmond 16
Man Who Fell to Earth, The (film) 4, 8n34, 17, 33, 79
Man Who Sold the World, The (album) 19, 23n72, 67n7, 77, 81n7, 82n50
Mapplethorpe, Robert 41, 52n1
market liberalism 28
Martyn, John 27, 30, 34
masks 30, 33
Matthew (Saint) 82n13
Max-Schmeling-Halle concert 78–79, 83n75
McLeod, Ken 22n57
melodious music 32
Merrick, John 8n37, 79; *see also Elephant Man, The* (play)
metamorphosis 20
method acting 33, 46, 47, 54n61
Metzger, Gustav 76, 82n36
Middle Ages 14, 53n47, 80
Middleton, Richard 28
Milton, John 53n16
mime 18, 33, 37n96
minimalism 18
Minotaur 19, 23n69
Mishima, Yukio 3
Mitchell, Joni 30
modernists: Burroughs and late 61; Eliot 43, 61, 62, 67n26, 68n38; idea of the singer-songwriter as genius 35n22; Joyce 61
mod imagery 18
Monkees 36n84
monsters: ambiguity of 17; anxiety produced by 15, 21n4; bestial humans 14; Bowie as 14, 17–20; as breach of law and nature 4, 15, 21n4; Canguilhem on 4, 13–16, 21n4; Carroll on 19; Cohen on 4, 5, 16; conjoined twins

on 68n43; soul 18, 33, 64, 68n54; transcendent 60; transgressive 4, 5, 17; *see also* art/artwork; rock music
musical authenticity 29
music hall 18
'My Death' (Brel song) 81n3
mysticism: Bowie's interest in 77; Gnosticism 77; Hermetic Qabalah 45, 48, 53n47, 56n116, 77, 82n52; Holy Grail 54n48, 68n33; Kabbalah 53n47, 77; Western esoteric tradition of 53n47; *see also* occult
mythology: Bowie's writing influenced by 62; the Griffin 21n4; Minotaur 19, 23n69; of Nazis 45, 54n48, 68n33; Pegasus 21n4; of rock culture 29; Siegfried in German 56n112; Tree of Life 48, 53–54n47, 55n98

Nabokov, Vladimir 41, 52n2
Naked Lunch (Burroughs) 65
narcissism xi, 31, 35n29
National Front 46–47, 54n66
nationalism 54n61
National Socialism *see* Nazis
nature 4, 15, 20, 21n4
Nazis: anti-semitism of 54n61; artistic props used by 41; Bowie's fascination with 45, 54n48; Goebbels use of media 54n48; Himmler's quest for Holy Grail 54n48, 68n33; ideology of 45; imagery of 45; Isolar world tour (1976) and 41, 50; mythology of 45; Nuremberg rallies 5, 47–48, 50, 55n94; occult and 45; Operation Fortitude against 54n51; paganism of 49; 'Quicksand' (song) on 45, 53–54n47, 68n33, 77, 81n3; racial purity vision of 51; "resurgence of interest in" 46; Speer's architecture 54n48; stagecraft of 41, 51; 'Station to Station' (song) and mindset of 49; symbols of 45; theatricality of 41; Third Reich 50; totalitarian mindset of 45; *Triumph of the Will* 48, 50, 55n94; on Weimar Republican decadence 48
necessity 7, 75–76
Neu (band) 22n43, 50, 69n74
New Critics 43
Newley, Anthony 18, 22n42
New York Times 2
Next Day, The (album) 78, 81n3, 83n59
'Next Day, The' (song) 78, 81n3
Nietzsche, Friedrich: on the abyss 51; on *agape* 73; antichrist of 74; on authenticity

as 14; conditions for producing 15; Derrida on 4, 14, 16; desire for 17; difference between humans and 13, 15; as dystopia portents 16; Eaton on 44; embracing 80–81; English common law on 13, 21n2; Foucault on 4, 13–16, 21n4, 21n22; framework for thinking about structure of 14–16; *Frankenstein* xiii, 14; the future and 16–17; gender of 18; vs. gods 14, 20; Hanafi on 13; hermaphrodites and 14, 16, 18; hopefulness of 4, 14, 16–17; human/animal hybridity and 18; Minotaur 19, 23n69; Mr. Hyde 14, 19; non-human hybrids as 15, 21n4; pointing to place of sacred in world without God 16, 17; in popular culture 17; "privileged" 18; psychoanalysis and 4, 13; of Ravenna 80, 83n87; Saint Augustine on 16; scary 17; science as creator/destroyer of 14, 15, 18; sexuality and 5; template for outsider in social theory 13; value of 17; vampires 4, 14, 17, 79; werewolf 14; who laugh at the law 1; Ziggy Stardust as 76; zombie 46; *see also* aliens
monstrare 16
monstrosity 8n37, 15, 18–19, 21n19
monstrousness 15, 19, 21n19
moral attitude 45
moral boundaries 43
moral character 49
moral defects 42, 44, 51, 53n16
moralism 6, 42–43, 45, 52n13, 53n15
morality 41, 43–45, 49, 51
moral knowledge 43–44
moral law 43
moral literature 53n17
moral selves 43, 44, 79
Morley, Paul 68n59
Mott the Hoople (band) 36n62
Mozart, Wolfgang Amadeus 2–3, 50
Murray, Shaar 8n24, 8n38, 22n66, 37n86
music: art rock 64; authenticity in 29; black American 18; blues 29; cacophonous 32; classical 50; cult of repetition in 76; disco 51; discordant 18, 33, 65; electronic 51, 69n74, 79; folk 18, 29–30, 36n52, 77; funk 18, 51, 64, 68n54; futuristic 48; grunge 29; hip hop 29; jazz 29; Kant on 68n43; melodious 32; music hall 18; Nietzsche on 68n43; operatic approach to 19; pop 76; as prophecy 3; psychobilly 37n94; punk 29, 37n94, 54n66, 64–65; 75; rockabilly 37n94; Schopenhauer

as a philosophical idea 35n25; Bowie's interest in 73–74, 79, 81n7; on Christianity 73; on compassion 74, 82nn15–16; on creativity 74; Critchley on 83n68; elitist, self-loving 'higher man' of 74; *Gay Science* (Nietzsche) 83n68; on God 83n68; immoralist ethics of 82n15; on life 73–74; on music 68n43; perspectivism of 74, 82n10; on self-preservation 74; Thin White Duke on 47; *Thus Spoke Zarathustra* (Nietzsche) 82n15; 'tough love' of 74
Night Porter, The (film) 46
non-human hybrids 15, 21n4, 84n92
norms 7, 28–29, 75
nostalgia 20, 48
Nova Express (Burroughs) 60, 61, 63
Nuremberg rallies 5, 47–48, 50, 55n94
Nussbaum, Martha 82n15

Oblique Strategies cards 65–66, 69n70
occult: Burroughs' and Bowie's interest in 59; Crowley and 53–54n47, 56n113, 67n7, 77; Hermetic Qabalah 45, 48, 53n47, 56n116, 77, 82n52; Kabbalah 53n47, 77; Nazi ideology and 45; tarot 67n24; Western esoteric tradition of 53n47
Odam, Norman Carl 37n94
Offenbach, Jacques 50
'Oh, You Pretty Things' (song) 73, 81n9
Oliver (musical) 22n42
O'Neill, Terry 83n84
ontology 7, 73, 78–80
opacity 3, 43, 49–50, 64–65
Operation Fortitude 54n51
Operation Overlord (D-Day) 54n51
Orff, Carl 50
originality 31–32, 36n71, 36n74
Orwell, George 5, 45, 53n22, 64
otherness 7, 33, 73, 74, 79, 81
Outside (album) 5, 69n71
outsiders: Aladdin Sane as 4; aliens as 4, 17; Bauman's *stranger* theory on 4; difference of 4; fan relationships and Bowie's role as 3, 8n19; freaks as 4; Girard's *scapegoat* theory on 4; Legendary Stardust Cowboy as 37n94; Pierrot as 4; in social theory 4, 13, 21n6; Thin White Duke as 4; vampires as 4, 17; Ziggy Stardust as 4

paganism 49
paintings 42, 76
Pasolini, Pier Paolo 46

Paul (Saint) 50
pedagogic/moral case for art/artwork 44
Peellaert, Guy 80
Pegasus 21n4
Perfect Moment, The (exhibition) 52n1
performance authenticity 28–29
personas: Aladdin Sane xi, 4, 8n38, 19, 32, 37n86; crafting and performing of 76; death of 76, 82n38; discussion of 32–34; fans' familiarity with Bowie's 2; Halloween Jack 4, 32; otherness of 33, 76; Pierrot 4, 32, 52; plastic soul-boy 32; Thomas Jerome Newton 33, 79; *see also* Thin White Duke; Ziggy Stardust
perspectivism 74, 82n10
Phillips, David 29
philosophical romanticism 28, 35n25
philosophy of art: art, ethics, and 42; autonomism 6, 42–43; immoralism 6, 43–45, 49, 51, 82n15; moralism 6, 42–43, 45, 52n13, 53n15
Picasso, Pablo 3
Picture of Dorian Gray, The (Wilde) 53n17
Pierrot 4, 32, 52
Piss Christ (artwork) 41, 52n3
plastic soul-boy 32
Playboy Magazine 46, 54n61, 55n70
political utopia 31
politics 30, 45–46, 50–51, 75
Pontius Pilate 55n97
pop music 76
popular culture 2, 3, 17
pose 19, 27, 35n22
postcolonial theory 4, 43
posthuman 7, 79–81
postmodern age 20
postmodernism 28, 35n22
postmodern record 8n20
postmodern rock star 3, 28, 35n22
power: "anxious reflection" on, on *Young Americans* album 47; art, ethics, and 5; attitude of Bowie's artwork and 49; and Burroughs' ideas on language as a virus 67n16; of the Christian church 78; desire for 49, 51; exploration of 50; in leader/follower relationship 5, 45–50; love of 47, 50; Nazis' dramatisation of 45; 'Quicksand' (song) on Hitler's 45; racial 49; of rock stars, Bowie on 47; 'Station to Station' album and theme of 49–50; and Thin White Duke tour 48
pre-queer 20
Presley, Elvis 20
pretension, new school of 28

private self 29, 30, 35n29
proto-punk 32
psyche 3, 15, 20; *see also* 'soul'
psychoanalysis 4, 13
psychobilly music 37n94
public self 29–30, 35n29
punk music 29, 37n94, 54n66, 64–65, 75
punks, swastikas worn by 47, 54n66

queer 19, 20; *see also* gay; homosexuality
queer sensibility 19
queer theory 4
'Quicksand' (song) 45, 53–54n47, 68n33, 77, 81n3

racial power 49
racial purity 51
Radioactivity (Kraftwerk album) 48
Razinsky, Hili 44
real/fake 28; *see also* fakery
realist art 80
reality 6, 14, 28, 30–32, 34, 61
Redmond, Sean 8n19
Reich, Wilhelm 3
Reisch, George 30
Renaissance 14, 53n47
repressed desire 48
Richards, Keith 27, 34, 34n1
Riefenstahl, Leni 48, 50, 55n94
Ring (Wagner) 41, 52n4, 56n112
Rise and Fall of Ziggy Stardust and the Spiders from Mars (album): dystopias explored in 5; 'Five Years' on 77; as a postmodern record 8n20; 'Rock 'n' Roll Suicide' on 82n14, 82n38; 'Starman' on 3, 8n26; *see also* Ziggy Stardust
ritual suicide, serial 76
robots 15; *see also* androids; cyborgs
robust immoralism 44
rockabilly music 37n94
Rock Against Racism movement 56n106
rock culture 29
rock music: artificiality of 19, 22n57, 30; authenticity and 5; Bowie's artwork challenging notions of 51; *Cock Rock* music 19, 22n55; constructed nature of 34; cult of repetition in 76; glam rock music 64; Krautrock 18, 33; 'masculinist subculture' in British 19; 'socially oppositional status' of 29; *see also* rock 'n' roll
rock 'n' roll: authenticity in 29; from black America 18; Bowie on 68n52; Critchley on 63–64; cut-ups and 6, 59, 67n3;

excess in 47; as a form of expression 2; leader/follower relationship in 50; Nuremberg rallies and 47–48; Thin White Duke on Hitler and 47
'Rock 'n' Roll Suicide' (song) 82n14, 82n38
Roeg, Nicholas, *The Man Who Fell to Earth* 4, 8n34, 17, 33, 79
Rolling Stone (magazine) 36n54, 60, 62, 68n38
Rolling Stones (band): Charlie Watts 34n1; 'Diamond Dogs' (song) and 64, 68n59; Mick Jagger 46, 59, 67n9; Keith Richards 27, 34, 34n1; as their own tribute band 34n1
romanticism 28, 35n25, 35n26
Ronson, Mick xi, 64
Rossinow, Douglas 30
Rousseau, Jean Jacques 35n25
Ruskin, John 42, 53n15

sacred 4, 16–17, 20, 21n28, 21n29
Saint Claire, Ericson 33
Salinger, J.D. 35n11
Salisbury, Joyce 80
Salo (film) 46
Sartre, Jean-Paul 35n25
Sauchelli, Andrea 44
Savage, Jon 8n20, 28
scapegoat 4, 21n6
scary monsters 17
Scary Monsters (album) 17, 21n34, 32, 69n71, 81n3
'Scary Monsters (And Super Creeps)' (song) 17, 21n34
Scheler, Max 74
Schmidt, Peter 69n70
Schopenhauer, Arthur 68n43
science 14, 15, 18, 22n46, 80
science fiction 33, 59, 67n24
Scorsese, Martin 55n97
Scott, Tony, *The Hunger* 4, 8n36, 17
self: alienation of 28; 'artistic' 29; Burroughs on sovereign 61; Carson on love and 81; community and 35n29; Foucault on care for the 84n101; metaphorical killing of 76; moral selves 43, 44, 79; ontology and 7, 73, 79; otherness privileged over 79, 81; paring back of 74, 77; performing the 'other' as "authentic" 30; private 29, 30, 35n29; public 29–30, 35n29; reinvention of 4, 5, 18; transcendence of 75; unselfing 77
self-creation 5, 30

self-deification 74
self-effacement 74, 77, 79
selfhood 7, 29, 74
self-preservation 74
self-reverence 74
sensual immediacy 63
Serano, Julia 22n64
Serrano, Andres 41, 52n3
sex 22n46, 59, 80
'Sex and the Church' (song) 78, 83n61
Sex Pistols (band) 54n66
sexual identity 19
sexuality: ambiguity about 18–20; Bowie's 19–20, 81n5; cis-sexuality 19, 22n64; *Cock Rock* music and 22n55; *Diamond Dogs* album and 65; heterosexuality 19, 20, 22n63; homosexuality 19, 22n52; monsters and 5
Shaft (film) 68n54
Shakespeare, William, *The Tempest* 55n101
Sheeran, Ed 78
Shelley, Mary xiii, 14, 35n26
Shelley, Percy Bysshe 35n26
Sid Vicious 54n66
Siegfried (Wagner) 56n112
'Silly Boy Blue' (song) 77
Siouxsie and the Banshees (band) 54n66
situationism 31
Slick, Earl 48
social norms 7, 28–29, 75
social theory 4, 13, 21n6, 67n16
'soul' 6, 15, 20, 29, 30, 50; *see also* psyche
soul music 18, 33, 64, 68n54
Space Oddity (album) 31, 36n63, 36n68, 36n69, 62, 68n33
Speer, Albert 54n48
spirituality 77
spontaneity 60
stagecraft 5, 41, 48, 49, 51
'Starman' (song) 3, 8n26
Station to Station (album): aesthetic properties of 51; Alomar's work on 54n69, 69n71; autonomism and 43; Lester Bangs on 49; and cocaine struggles 56n116; as an exorcism 56n116; 'Golden Years' on 19, 50, 51; operatic approach to music on 22n60; 'Station to Station' on 48–50, 53n47, 55n101, 56n113, 77; and the sublime 51; Thin White Duke and 37n89; Thin White Duke tour and 9n53, 42, 52n9; Tree of Life and 48, 53–54n47; 'Word on a Wing' on 56n116, 77, 82n53

'Station to Station' (song) 48–50, 53n47, 55n101, 56n113, 77
Station to Station tour 55n76; *see also* Thin White Duke tour
Stevenson, Robert Louis 14, 19
Stockhausen, Karl Heinz 3, 50, 64
stranger 4, 21n6
the sublime 9n55, 28, 41, 43, 51, 64
'Subterreaneans' (song) 66, 69n77
suicide 45, 65, 76
Summer of Love 31
'Sunday' (song) 77, 83n54
'Supermen, The' (song) 23n72, 77
surrealism 48
swastika 47, 54n66
'Sweet Thing' (song) 19, 33, 63, 64
'Sweet Thing/Candidate/Sweet Thing (Reprise)' (triptych) 33, 63–65, 69n68
symbols, Nazis set of 45

taboo 80
tarot 67n24
Taylor, Charles 29–31, 35n29
technological dreams 63
Tempest, The (Shakespeare) 55n101
Terminator, The (film) 15, 21n13
Thin White Duke: aesthetics and 5–6; art, ethics, and 5–6, 41–42; avant-garde and 32; Bowie on 46–47; cocaine and 47; Critchley on Stockholm interview 54n61; on decadence 47; descriptions of 46; as distant 5, 32, 34; dystopian futures and 45; Edward VIII and 46; Bowie's emotional investment in 33; on fascist leader for Britain 54n61; flirting with fascism 5, 33, 41, 45–49, 54n61; on freedom 47; German expressionism and 33; German modernism and 32; 'Heil and Farewell' incident and 54n60; on Hitler and rock 'n' roll concerts 47; interviews of 46–47, 54n61, 55n70; on Isolar world tour (1976) 41; Krautrock and 33; leader/ follower relationship of fans with 45–50; as mad aristocrat 46; soul music and 33; stagecraft of 5, 41, 48, 49, 51; *Station to Station* album and 37n89; Thomas Jerome Newton and 33; totalitarian mindset of 33, 54n61; Ziggy Stardust and 46
Thin White Duke tour 5, 9n53, 42, 48–50, 52n9; *see also* Station to Station tour
Third Reich 50
Thomas Jerome Newton 33, 79
Thus Spoke Zarathustra (Nietzsche) 82n15
Tibetan Buddhism 77

'Time' (song) 62, 81n3
time travel 59, 67n6
time warp 61
Tin Machine (album) 78, 83n63
Tolkien, J. R. R. 56n106
Tolstoy, Leo 42, 53n15
Tonight (album) 77–78, 83n57
totalitarianism 45, 47, 49
Townshend, Pete 76
transcendence 75, 78
transcendent music 60
transgender 81n5
transgression 43, 50, 75; *see also* estrangement
transgressive art 4, 5, 17, 41, 49
transgressive homosexuality 22n52
transgressive music 4, 5, 17
trans theory 4
Tree of Life 48, 53–54n47, 55n98
Trilling, Lionel 28
Triumph of the Will (Riefenstahl film) 48, 50, 55n94
truth 1, 5, 27–34, 65, 82n10
Tzara, Tristan 59

Übermensch 32
Un Chien Andalou (film) 48, 55n87
unconditional love 73, 79
unconscious, collective 62
undecidability 20
unheimlich 17
unity 30, 32, 33, 50
unselfing 77
utopia, political 31

vampires 4, 14, 17, 79
Velvet Underground (band) 33
Vollmer, Joan 67n5
vulnerability 51, 64, 77

Wagner, Richard 41, 50, 52n4, 56n112
Waldrep, Shelton 19
Ward, Brian 80
Warhol, Andy 30, 31, 35n22
'Warszawa' (song) 66, 69n75
Waste Land, The (Eliot) 62, 67n26, 68n38
Watts, Charlie 34n1
Watts, Michael 19
'We Are Hungry Men' (song) 54n53

'We are the Dead' (song) 64
Weill, Kurt 50, 55n76
Weimar Republic 48
Weinstein, Deena 29
werewolf 14
'When I Live my Dream' (song) 68n33
White Light tour 9n53, 52n9; *see also* Thin White Duke tour
White Stains (Crowley) 53n47
the Who (band) 76
Wild Boys, The (Burroughs) 65, 67n8, 69n63
Wilde, Oscar 19, 22n41, 30, 53n17
'Wild Eyed Boy from Freecloud' (song) 31, 36n69
'Word on a Wing' (song) 56n116, 77, 82n53
Wordsworth, William 35n26
word-virus 6, 61, 67n16
World of David Bowie, The (album) 62, 77, 82n49

yearning 33, 75
Young, Neil 30
Young Americans (album): Alomar's work on 69n71; "anxious reflection" on power on 47; black American funk on 51; 'Fame' on 47, 55n80; plastic soul-boy persona and 32; release of 37n88; 'Young Americans' on 78, 83n73
'Young Americans' (song) 78, 83n73

Zappa, Frank 59, 67n3
Zarathustra 82n15
Ziggy Stardust: Aladdin Sane and 8n38, 32, 37n86; construction of 22n57, 33; death of 82n38; Bowie's emotional investment in 33; guitar playing by 19; highly sexualised camp of 19; as "Kabuki monster" 76; leader/follower relationship of fans with 50; as a messiah 32, 37n86, 45, 54n53; as proto-punk 32, 37n86, 76; Thin White Duke and 46; *see also Rise and Fall of Ziggy Stardust and the Spiders from Mars* (album)
Ziggy Stardust tour 81n3
Zizek, Slavoj 1
zombie 46

Printed in Great Britain
by Amazon

44124049R00071